The Complete Book

of

Victims' Rights

Debra J. Wilson, J.D.

ProSe Associates, Inc.
Highlands Ranch, Colorado

This book is designed to provide you with accurate information about the law so that you can deal more effectively with the legal situations that concern you. However, your own situation may be different from the ones described in this book. In addition, laws are subject to change and varying interpretations. As a result, this book is sold with the understanding that neither the author nor the publisher is engaged in rendering specific legal or other professional services to any individual.

The persons and events described in this book, while based in fact, are not directly related to any particular persons or events, and any similarity between the persons described herein and any persons living or dead is purely coincidental.

Published by:
ProSe Associates, Inc.
P.O. Box 4333
Highlands Ranch, Colorado 80126

Printed in the U.S.A.

10 9 8 7 6 5 4 3 2 1

ISBN: 0-9637285-1-2
Library of Congress Number: 95-68929

CONTENTS

INTRODUCTION

Compassion, sensitivity, respect, dignity, courtesy. These words are not often used in discussions of crime and the criminal justice system in the United States. However, in the last decade, many states have passed laws that strive to insure that when the victims of crime come into contact with the police, prosecutors, and the courts, they will in fact be treated with compassion, sensitivity, respect, dignity and courtesy.

The victims' rights movement is based on the perception, unfortunately often true, that in the business of catching criminals and obtaining convictions, the victims of crime are frequently overlooked. As state legislatures around the country recognize that the victims of crime are important to the criminal justice system, and that their cooperation is absolutely necessary, they have worked to grant the same kinds of rights and protections to the victims of crime that have long been guaranteed to those accused of crime. Additionally, the various states have enacted laws designed to help redress the financial, emotional and physical suffering of crime victims.

One of the best explanations for the passage of victims' rights laws is found in the 1981 preamble to the Nebraska Crime Victims and Witness Assistance Act:

> There is a need to develop methods to reduce the trauma and discomfort that victims of a crime and witnesses to a crime may experience because they often are further victimized by the criminal justice system.
> When a crime occurs the chief concern of law enforcement and prosecutors is to apprehend and punish the criminal and the needs of the victim are frequently forgotten.
> Victims are often isolated and receive little advice or care.
> Little thought is given to the schedules and obligations of witnesses who are required to appear in court.
> Witnesses must often wait a long time before giving their testimony, they don't understand the proceedings in which they are participating, and they

receive no information regarding the ultimate disposition of the case.

Many victims and witnesses are unaware of their rights and obligations.

Many people do not report crimes, and it is due to their disillusionment with the criminal justice system.

The information that a victim can supply the police is the single most important factor in determining whether a case will be solved, thus victim cooperation is absolutely essential to the detection and prosecution of crime.

Victim's rights acts and individual laws designed to protect victims seek to balance a system that has, in the past, focused solely on the rights of the accused. Consider:

- Criminal defendants have a constitutional right to a speedy trial. Now, in many states, victims have the right to a timely disposition of their cases as well.
- Criminal defendants have the right to be present at all the proceedings against them. Now, in many states, crime victims have the right to notice of all proceedings and the right to be present. This may include the right to notice of and participation in post conviction proceedings such as parole hearings. There was a time when these proceedings took place behind closed doors; offenders could be released without the victims of their crimes even knowing that they were back on the streets.
- Sentencing hearings were, at one time, devoted solely to the defendant, his or her needs, the proper punishment, and plans for rehabilitation. Now many states mandate that victims have the right to provide input and present evidence at sentencing. Victims need not remain faceless in the sentencing process and have the right to express their own needs and views to the court. Many states now require that a restitution order be a part of most sentences.
- A criminal defendant has the constitutional right to confront his or her accusers. However, new legislation has tempered this right. Young victims of crime may,

under some circumstances, be allowed to give their testimony outside the presence of the defendant.

- •Plea bargaining has traditionally been an agreement reached between the state and the criminal. In many states, victims are now granted the legal right to participate in the process, and even to make their views regarding a particular plea bargain known to the court.

- •Almost every state recognizes that some victims require special care and treatment, and have laws to protect victims of sexual offenses, victims of family violence, and children who are the victims of crime. For example, in addition to providing immediate medical care, most states provide referrals to appropriate counseling resources, and provide that communications between victim and counselor remain confidential and need not be divulged in court. The victims of family violence are afforded civil as well as criminal remedies and support services such as safe houses and advocates when they go to court. Mandatory arrest programs in many jurisdictions help ease some of the pressure faced by these victims. In most states, the victims of sexual assault have legal methods available to require their attackers undergo testing for the AIDS virus.

- •States now recognize a duty to financially assist the victims of crime and set aside public money for the compensation of the crime victims.

- •Victims are no longer just expected to show up and do what they are told. Many state laws mandate that victims have the right to information about the entire criminal justice process and their role in that process. Additionally, in many states the prosecutor's office is required to intercede, if necessary, with employers. Some states make it illegal to fire or penalize employees who must miss work because of required court attendance.

Victims' rights laws are of no use to crime victims and their families if they don't know about them. This book is designed to serve as a guide to the victims of crimes involved with the criminal justice system, their families, and others interested in victims' rights.

Crime victims and their families are urged to consult with the prosecutor or victim-witness coordinator in their jurisdiction to learn more about their rights.

My goal is to inform crime victims and their families of the type of treatment they should expect, regardless of whether there is a specific law on the books. Even if your state does not grant a particular right by law, such as the right to employer intercession or the right to be notified of the disposition of an appeal, the fact that other states do provide it should enable you to request that a particular service or particular information be provided. You are an essential participant in the criminal justice process. You have the right to be treated that way.

–Debra Wilson

CHAPTER 1

BETWEEN THE CRIME AND THE TRIAL

Victims' Rights in Investigations, Bail Decisions, Dispositions, and Plea Bargaining

Jim and Susan celebrated their anniversary with a late dinner in a new restaurant. The restaurant was in a refurbished warehouse, near the river. They finished dinner at about 11:30 PM, and their trip home took them through almost deserted city streets. When they stopped at a red light they were suddenly confronted by three young men, one of whom aimed a gun directly at Susan through the car window. The men demanded that they get out of their car, and the couple complied.

Once they were on the sidewalk, they were robbed. One of the men took Susan's purse and Jim's wallet. The man holding the gun on them then pointed it at Jim and pulled the trigger. Luckily the gun misfired, and the attackers panicked and fled in the couple's car. As soon as the trio drove away, Jim and Susan found an open convenience store and had the clerk call the police.

Jim and Susan were picked up by a patrol car and driven to the police station where they made their report. Then they got a ride home. They immediately canceled their credit cards, and the next day, contacted their insurance company and made arrangements to rent a car and change the locks on their house. Once they dealt with those details, they started wondering if the police were making any progress on their case. Do they have the right to information about the investigation of the crime?

In most cases, law enforcement personnel will voluntarily share information about case progress with victims. However, if sharing information would impede, hinder or jeopardize the ongoing investigation, they will not do so, and may withhold information.

Some states have laws which mandate that victims be kept reasonably informed of the status of the criminal investigation and major developments in the case. The following states have such laws: Connecticut, Delaware, Hawaii, Illinois, Maryland, Missouri, New Hampshire, North Dakota and South Carolina.

The following states go further, requiring that more specific information be provided to victims:

> *Colorado*: The victim has the right to the file number of his or her case, the phone number of the prosecutor assigned to the case, and the phone number of the investigating officer.
> *Ohio*: The victim is entitled to the case number and a phone number to call for information regarding the case.
> *Arizona*: The victim is given a number to call if he or she is not notified of an arrest within 30 days. Once the case is submitted for prosecution, the victim is entitled to receive the name, address and phone number of the prosecutor handling the case.
> *Michigan*: The victim is directed to call if there has been no notification of an arrest within 6 months.
> *Rhode Island*: The victim has the right to be notified, at the least, every three months of the status of the investigation.
> *Wyoming*: The victim has the right to the names, addresses and telephone numbers of the primary law enforcement officer and prosecutor assigned to investigate the case.

Will Jim and Susan automatically be notified if arrests are made in their case?

It is good practice for police departments and prosecutors to notify victims when an arrest has been made, but it is not mandated by law in every state. The following states provide that victims have the right to be notified when an arrest is made: Arizona, Connecticut, Colorado, Florida, Louisiana, Maryland, Montana, New York, Pennsylvania and West Virginia.

In Nebraska there is no law which mandates notification when an arrest is made, but a victim has the right to examine police records regarding arrests in the case.

The day after the crime, Jim and Susan were notified that the police had apprehended the carjackers within an hour of the attack on them. Each of them has been charged with carjacking, armed robbery and assault with intent to kill. Will Jim and Susan be notified if their assailants are released on bail?

Jim and Susan should tell the police officers and prosecutor handling the case that they wish to be notified if their attackers are released on bail or on their own recognizance. If they don't make their wishes known, they might not get word of the defendants' release. Some states do provide that victims have the right to this information, but it is usually necessary for the victim to affirmatively assert his or her rights.

The following states provide that the victim has the right to notice of the defendant's pretrial release: Connecticut, Illinois, Kentucky, Louisiana, Michigan, Montana, Rhode Island, Tennessee, Vermont, West Virginia, Wisconsin and Wyoming.

In the following states, the victim not only has the right to notice, but also the right to know the conditions of the defendant's release: Colorado, Delaware, Iowa, Nevada (in Nevada, the victim is entitled to know the amount of bail required) and North Dakota.

In the states of Arizona, Maryland, Missouri, South Carolina, South Dakota, Texas and West Virginia the victim has the right to notice of the bail hearing. In many of these states, the victim has the right to appear and address the court regarding bail. In the states of Mississippi and Texas, the court must consider the safety of the victim and the victim's family when setting bail. In Florida and New York the victim has the right to consult with the prosecutor regarding bail.

Jim and Susan realize that if their attackers looked at their driver's licenses, they may know where they live. They fear that if released on bail, the men arrested for this crime may try to harm

them, to keep them from testifying against them. Is there anything that they can do?

In every state, an attempt to intimidate a witness is a serious crime, and a person who tries to keep a witness from testifying may be punished quite severely, even if the witness is not actually harmed. Victims and witnesses are entitled to protection from harm by law enforcement personnel. Any individual who interferes with a witness while on bail faces additional criminal charges, as well as the possible revocation of his or her bail.

Some state laws provide special protection for victims or witnesses who have been threatened. In Arizona, Indiana, New Mexico, Michigan and Oregon, a prosecutor may move that a defendant's bail be revoked if the victim submits an affidavit that he or she has been subjected to acts or threats of violence or intimidation. In Arizona, if the prosecutor declines to act on the victim's request, the victim may petition the court directly for bail revocation.

In Ohio and Iowa, there is a civil remedy. If a victim or witness files an affidavit or verified complaint alleging harassment or intimidation, the court may issue a temporary restraining order or civil injunction against the offender, prohibiting such actions. A violation of the order may be punished as contempt of court, with fines and/or imprisonment. In Pennsylvania, the Court may enter similar protective orders that the defendant maintain a prescribed distance from the victim or the witness.

About two months before the trial was scheduled to begin, Jim and Susan met with the prosecutor assigned to their case. They discussed their testimony and the prosecutor told them that the case was strong. Both Jim and Susan picked the defendants out of a line up, and all had been caught in the stolen car, with Jim and Susan's property. However, as they were preparing to leave, the prosecutor mentioned that he expected the defense would want to plea bargain the case. In that event, he said, Jim and Susan wouldn't have to testify at a trial. What did the prosecutor mean by the term "plea bargain," and what effect would it have on the case?

A plea bargain is an agreement between the prosecutor and the defendant/ In a plea bargain, the two sides to the criminal prosecution strike a deal. The prosecutor agrees to drop one or more charges, or reduce the charges, in exchange for the defendant's plea of guilty to the remaining or reduced charges.

In some cases, the prosecutor may agree to make a recommendation that the defendant receive a lighter sentence, or probation, in return for a plea of guilty. In other cases, the defendant agrees to testify against co-defendants in return for reduced or dismissed charges.

The benefit to the defendant is that he or she is not convicted of, or punished for, every crime that could be charged. The benefit to the prosecutor is that the state is not put to the time and expense of a trial, and the state is guaranteed a conviction, there is no chance of a verdict of not guilty.

However, in many cases, victims of the defendant's criminal actions are not considered or consulted. Victims can be left feeling that the defendant is not being made accountable for all his or her wrongdoing.

What would a plea bargain mean in this particular case?

The prosecutor would have many options in a case like this one. The prosecutor might agree to drop one or two charges, in exchange for a guilty plea on the one remaining charge. He might reduce the assault with intent to murder to simple assault or reduce the carjacking charge to a charge of auto theft or reduce the armed robbery charge to simple theft. He might do this for one defendant in return for testimony against the others.

Their case seems almost airtight, and Jim and Susan don't mind going to court. In fact, they want to meet their attackers in court and see that justice is done. Can they tell the prosecutor that they absolutely refuse to allow a plea bargain in their case?

No. The decision to prosecute a crime and the decision as to what crime to charge is the prosecutor's. The victim or victims of a crime may not direct the prosecution, nor do they have any redress if the prosecutor makes decisions that they don't agree with, including the decision to plea bargain the case.

Can Jim and Susan at least meet with the prosecutor and let him know that they oppose a plea bargain?

Yes. Any good prosecutor will confer with the victims of a crime before entering into a plea bargain, to get their input. To insure that prosecutors consider the wishes and concerns of crime victims, many state have laws that require the prosecutor to inform the victims of a crime (some states limit this to the victims of violent crime) of his or her intention to enter into plea negotiations with the defendant or defendants. In some states the victim may request a conference with the prosecutor to discuss the proposed plea, and state his or her concerns and or objections.

The following states require that the prosecutor notify the victim of a possible plea agreement before it is entered into: Idaho, Illinois, North Carolina, South Carolina, Tennessee, Texas and Wyoming.

The following states require that upon the victim's request, the prosecutor confer with him or her regarding a plea bargain, or give the victim the opportunity to comment regarding a plea agreement: Arizona, Colorado, Delaware, Florida, Hawaii, Kansas, Kentucky, Louisiana, Maine, Michigan, Minnesota, New Hampshire, New Mexico, Montana, New York, Pennsylvania, Utah and West Virginia. In South Dakota, the victim has the right to provide the prosecutor with written input regarding a possible plea agreement.

In the state of Louisiana, the victims have the right to retain their own lawyer, to confer with law enforcement and the prosecutor. In Louisiana, the victims could have their lawyer express their concerns to the prosecutor regarding any proposed disposition.

If Jim and Susan state their opposition, and the prosecutor still intends to go forward with a plea bargain, can they contact the court directly?

In some states the victim has the right to appear at a hearing that is scheduled for the presentation of a plea agreement to the court, and to state his or her opinion regarding the plea agreement.

Other statutes require that the prosecutor present the victims' position to the court. The court may reject the plea agreement, or refuse to follow the prosecutor's sentencing recommendation. In states without such legislation, the victims still have the right to be present in court, and can make their opinions known at sentencing, or in the pre-sentence investigation report.

The following states allow crime victims to appear at the hearing in which a negotiated plea will be presented to the court and state their opinion regarding the plea bargain: Arizona, (if the victim does not appear, the prosecutor must certify to the court that reasonable efforts were made to contact and confer with the victim. The prosecutor must inform the court of the victim's position regarding the plea bargain if it is known.) Colorado, and Minnesota, (although if the prosecutor is aware that the victim opposes the plea agreement, he or she must inform the court of the victim's objections.) In Connecticut and Missouri, the victim may present a statement regarding his or her losses to the court, prior to the acceptance of a negotiated plea. In South Dakota the prosecutor must inform the victim of the plea agreement and give the victim an opportunity to comment. Then, at the time the plea bargain is presented to the court, the prosecutor must disclose the victim's comments to the court. In New York, the court must consider the victim's views regarding the plea agreement.

Jim and Susan heard from a police detective that charges had been dismissed against one of the suspects. Are they entitled to an explanation as to why the prosecution against him was dropped?

In many states, Jim and Susan would be entitled, by law, to notification of the prosecutor's decision to drop charges, or for declining to charge a person arrested for the crime. The following states have such laws: Arizona, Colorado, Delaware, Kansas, Kentucky, Louisiana, Maryland, Michigan, Montana, New Hampshire, New York, and West Virginia. In Arizona, the victim may request a meeting with the prosecutor before the final decision is made. In New Jersey, the victim may submit a written victim impact statement for the prosecutor's review before he or she makes a formal decision as to whether or not charges will be filed. In Washington, the prosecutor is "encouraged" to notify the victim of the decision not to prosecute.

In states without such laws, the victims are certainly entitled to an explanation, and should request one, even if they are not allowed to have input into the decision.

Susan read in the newspaper about a program called "pre-trial diversion." It sounded a lot like plea bargaining to her. What is a "pre-trial diversion" and does she have the right to be notified if any of the defendants enter this program?

Pre-trial diversion is similar to plea bargaining in some ways. The prosecutor and the defendant agree that the criminal charges will be suspended, (or put on hold) for a period of time, usually six months to two years. The defendant will be required to meet certain criteria during that time. The requirements might be to pay restitution to the victims, to complete his or her education, drug and alcohol treatment. Most importantly, the defendant must stay out of trouble during the diversionary period. If the defendant successfully completes this probationary period, the charges against him or her will be dropped. If not, the charges will be reinstated, and he or she will be prosecuted. Many pretrial diversion programs are available only to first time offenders.

In the following states, the victim has the right to consult with the prosecutor regarding any decision to offer a defendant a pre-trial diversion program: Arizona, Colorado, Delaware, Florida, Kentucky, Michigan, Minnesota, Montana, Oregon and West Virginia. In Connecticut the victim is entitled to notice that the defendant has been offered the option of participating in a pre-trial diversion program.

Notification of Rights and Services

When the police and prosecutors begin an investigation of a crime, many state laws require them to provide the victims with prompt notification of their rights. The requirements vary from state to state, but in most states victims should be informed of:

•The right to request and receive restitution
•The right to apply for victim compensation funds
•The provisions of the state crime victim's bill of rights
•Information regarding witness services and witness fees
•Information regarding crisis services
•"Son of Sam" laws
•The availability of emergency and medical services. If the victims need immediate medical attention, they are not to be detained unreasonably by law enforcement.
•The telephone number of the victim and witness advocate.

CHAPTER 2

GOING TO COURT

Jessica came home from work early because she had a dental appointment. She noticed that her front door was unlocked, and chided herself for being careless that morning. However, when she walked into her den, she came face to face with a burglar, who looked as surprised to see her as she was to see him. He pushed her aside and ran out of her house, carrying her VCR under his arm. When Jessica went to her bedroom, she saw that it had been ransacked. She quickly checked her top dresser drawer and discovered that the $400 she had put there two days earlier was missing.

Jessica called the police and was able to give them a good description of the burglar. Within minutes, he was picked up at a bus stop, still carrying Jessica's VCR. Jessica's money was gone, although the police found about $400 worth of cocaine in the burglar's possession. A few hours after the arrest, Jessica was called to the police station, where she identified the burglar in a line up. She is going to be called as a witness at the trial.

The prosecutor told Jessica that she wouldn't be needed until the preliminary hearing, then mentioned something about an arraignment, but said she wouldn't have to attend. Jessica is very confused about the proceedings, and wants to know where she fits in. What should she do?

Jessica should feel free to ask the prosecutor, or the victim-witness coordinator in the prosecutor's office, any question that she has. Many states require that the prosecutor take time with crime victims and explain the procedural steps of a criminal prosecution to them. The prosecutor should explain the role of the victim in each step, and let the victim know what will be expected of him or her. This is good practice in any state, and the following states have made it a legal requirement: Delaware, Florida, Kansas, Louisiana, Michigan, Mississippi, Missouri, Montana, New Hampshire, New

Jersey, New York, North Dakota, South Carolina, Tennessee, Utah and West Virginia.

In the following states, the victim has the right to request a conference with the prosecutor prior to trial, to discuss his or her testimony, or any questions or concerns about the criminal justice process: Arizona, Colorado, Delaware, Michigan, Nevada (in felony cases) South Carolina, Texas, Utah and Wyoming.

In South Dakota the law states that the victim has the right to a clear explanation of what particular charges mean, and what is necessary for a conviction. The victim also has the right to be prepared as a witness, which includes being given information regarding the basic rules of evidence.

Jessica's friend Ruth was a witness to a car accident, and the judge made her sit outside the courtroom until it was time for her to testify. Jessica wants to hear all the evidence in the case. Can she stay in the courtroom for all the proceedings?

In many court proceedings, lawyers tell the judge that they want to "invoke the rule." They are referring to a rule that allows the parties to a lawsuit to have anyone who is going to testify at the trial removed from the courtroom, until they have given their testimony. This is also known as sequestering witnesses, and this is what happened in Ruth's case.

There is a logical reason for this practice. It prevents witnesses from shaping or changing their testimony based on what they heard another witness say. Unfortunately, as a result of this practice, the victims of crime are often forced to sit in a conference room or a hallway during important parts of the trial, not knowing what is occurring.

Some states have passed legislation that exempts crime victims from this rule and allows them to remain in the courtroom at all times, even if they are going to be called to give testimony. Other state laws provide that victims have the right to attend the trial and any other proceeding that the accused has the right to attend. The following states have such laws: Arizona, Arkansas, California, Colorado, Connecticut, Delaware, Florida, Georgia (at the judge's discretion), Illinois, Indiana, Kansas, Louisiana, Maryland, Missouri,

New Hampshire, New Mexico, Oklahoma, Oregon, South Dakota and Wyoming. In Alabama, the victim not only has the right to be present, he or she, (or the victim's representative) has the right to be seated at counsel table with the prosecutor. In Michigan, the victim may be excluded until he or she testifies. In the state of Washington, prosecutors are encouraged to schedule the testimony of victims early in the proceedings so that they may remain in the courtroom to hear the rest of the evidence in the case.

Many of these laws do allow the exclusion of the victim if the victim's presence would interfere with the defendant's right to a fair trial, or would violate the defendant's constitutional rights. In California and Illinois, the prosecutor may have the victim removed, if the victim's presence would hinder the prosecution of the case. And even in states that grant the victim the right to be present, victims who become disruptive or who refuse to abide by the standards set by the judge for courtroom behavior may be excluded.

About a week after the crime, Jessica started noticing the same car driving slowly by her house several times a day. Nothing else has happened, but she's afraid it might be the defendant or a friend of his. What should Jessica do?

Jessica should contact the prosecutor's office at once. Witnesses and victims have the right to be free from intimidation and protected by law enforcement. The following states specifically mandate witness and victim protection, and most of them require that victims be informed of the steps that they can take to receive protection from intimidation: Alaska, Arkansas, Colorado, Delaware, Florida, Hawaii, Kansas, Louisiana, Maryland, Massachusetts, Michigan, Mississippi, Missouri, Montana, Nebraska, Nevada, New Hampshire, New Jersey, New Mexico, New York, North Carolina, Oklahoma, Pennsylvania, South Carolina, Utah, Vermont and Wyoming.

Jessica is nervous about going to court. She doesn't want to encounter the defendant or his family in the hallways. What should she do?

She should be provided with a safe waiting area. Many state laws provide that there must be a separate pretrial waiting area for victims, where they won't come into contact with the defendant, his or her family members, or the defendant's witnesses. If space for a separate area is not available, the court is to provide other safeguards to minimize contact between the victim and the defendant or the defendant's family or witnesses, before, during and after the trial.

Jessica should discuss the layout of the courthouse and waiting areas with the prosecutor or the victim/witness coordinator ahead of time. If necessary, Jessica should ask for an escort to and from her car as well.

Jessica was told that the trial would occur about two months after the arrest, but her case has been put off twice, and it's been seven months since the burglary. Is there anything Jessica can do to try to get this over with, as soon as possible?

The United States Constitution and state constitutions guarantee criminal defendants the right to a speedy trial, but, until lately, there was no such guarantee for crime victims. Now, many states recognize that victims also suffer when justice is delayed again and again. Those states have enacted speedy trial laws that work on behalf of victims.

In some states, the victim has the right to be informed if the parties are requesting that the case be delayed or "continued." The victim has the right to appear at the hearing for the continuance request and comment on that request. Other states simply guarantee that crime victims have the right to a prompt resolution or disposition of their cases.

The following states have "speedy trial" provisions for the benefit of all crime victims: Arizona, California, Colorado, Florida, Maryland, Massachusetts, Michigan, Missouri, Nebraska, North Dakota, South Carolina, Tennessee, Utah and Wisconsin.

Some states provide that priority be given to cases in which the victims or material witnesses are young children or elderly. The following states have "speedy trial" provisions for very young or very old victims: California, Delaware, Kentucky, Oregon, Rhode Island, Utah, Washington and Wisconsin.

Minnesota law provides that, upon the victim's request, the prosecutor should make a demand that the trial begin within 60 days of the demand.

In Oregon and Wyoming, the court is directed to consider the victim when setting or resetting the date of the trial.

On one occasion, Jessica appeared at court, but no one was there. Her case had been continued and no one had told her. Isn't she entitled to some sort of notice?

Yes. Many states provide in their statutes or constitutional amendments providing for the rights of crime victims that victims and witnesses who have been scheduled to attend a hearing should be notified as soon as possible of any scheduling changes. Victims and witnesses should keep in touch with the prosecutor, or with the victim/witness coordinator in the prosecutor's office to be kept up to date on the scheduling of hearings.

To make things easier on the prosecutor, as well as on oneself, the victim should inform the prosecutor's office where and how he or she may be reached at all times. In addition to leaving home and work numbers, it would be a good idea to leave the number of friends or relatives who usually know of the victim's whereabouts.

In addition to the stress of waiting for her case to go to trial, Jessica has been without the use of her VCR, since it was taken from the burglar by the police. It's going to be used as evidence in the case. Couldn't Jessica get it back and promise to bring it the day of the trial?

Not if the prosecutor needs to produce the VCR at trial. If that is the case, the police will need to establish a "chain of custody", so they can prove in court that the VCR that Jessica identifies as belonging to her was the same one the police recovered from the defendant.

However, Jessica should consult with the prosecutor handling her case to see if a photograph of the VCR can be substituted for the machine itself. Many states have laws which provide that victim's property should be promptly returned unless there is a compelling reason for retaining it. If there is no substantial need for the property as evidence, many state laws allow the court to order that a photograph be substituted for the actual property. A crime victim should always enquire of the prosecutor if the property is necessary as evidence.

Victims should not rely on the police to notify them when they may retrieve their property, because they will retain it as a matter of course, unless the prosecutor instructs them otherwise.

The following states have provisions for the substitution of photographs for the actual property, if there is no need to retain the property for evidentiary reasons: Arizona, Florida, Kentucky, Michigan, North Carolina, South Carolina, South Dakota, Virginia and Washington.

The following states have laws that provide that prosecutors should see that personal property is returned to the victim as soon as possible, once it is no longer needed as evidence: Arkansas, California, Colorado, Connecticut, Delaware, Hawaii, Idaho, Illinois, Louisiana, Maryland, Massachusetts, Montana, Missouri, Nebraska, Nevada, New Mexico, New Hampshire, New Jersey, New York, North Dakota, Oklahoma, Pennsylvania, Rhode Island, Tennessee, Texas, Utah, West Virginia, Wisconsin, and Wyoming. Vermont law provides that victim advocates in that state should assist a victim seeking the return of his or her property.

A victim is not entitled to the return of his or her property if it is contraband (unlawful to possess), if it is subject to forfeiture, or if its ownership is in dispute.

The prosecutor says that Jessica's case will last at least two days, and she will have to remain available to testify until she is released by the court. Jessica is going to miss two days of work. Can she refuse to testify unless she receives compensation for her lost wages?

No. Witnesses in criminal cases can be compelled to attend court and give their evidence through the subpoena power of the court. A subpoena is a direct order from the court to a witness to appear in court at a certain day and time, and to remain available until released. Failure to obey a subpoena may result in incarceration or fines for contempt of court. A subpoena creates a legal obligation that may not be ignored, even if it means inconvenience or financial hardship.

Almost all states provide for compensation for witnesses, but it is usually meager. Payments of $10 to $15 per day are the norm, and many states pay much less for court attendance. Mileage is usually paid to witnesses who must travel from out of state or from a different county in the same state. Witnesses usually collect their fees by submitting a statement or affidavit after their court attendance.

Because of the time, expense and inconvenience of traveling to another state to testify, out of state witnesses are, in almost all states, entitled to be paid a witness fee as well as mileage at the time that they receive a subpoena or other order directing them to appear in court.

Most statutes enacting victim's rights or providing for victim services require prosecutors or law enforcement officials to inform crime victims if they are entitled to witness fees, and assist them in applying for them.

Jessica's boss was very unhappy when he learned she would be missing two days of work. She's afraid she might be fired. But if she doesn't attend court, she could be arrested. What should she do?

Jessica should ask the prosecutor about laws that protect witnesses from employer retaliation. In many states, it is illegal to fire an employee for missing work for required court attendance. For example, a Florida law provides that if a person is fired because he or she was absent from work while obeying a subpoena, the employee may sue the employer for his or her actual damages (such as lost wages and expenses incurred in obtaining other employment), attorneys fees and punitive damages.

Not all states provide such strong protection. However, most states with victim's rights acts mandate that prosecutors or law enforcement intercede with employers, explain to the employer that the victim's cooperation is necessary for successful prosecution of the case, and attempt to insure that the victim's loss of pay or benefits will be minimal. Some state laws also provide that prosecutors should try to minimize scheduling conflicts when setting interviews or court appearances.

In addition to missing work, Jessica lost the money she had earmarked for her utility and insurance payments. She is afraid to contact her creditors, because she doesn't think they will believe her. Can she get some help in explaining her circumstances?

Yes. The prosecutor or police officers in charge of her case should be able to verify for creditors the circumstances of her loss. Many states, such as Colorado, Florida, Massachusetts, Missouri, Montana, New York, South Carolina, West Virginia and Wyoming now provide that, upon request, the prosecutor must intercede with creditors, and explain to creditors the reason for the victim's temporary financial problems.

Jessica has heard of cases in which the jury is out for days. Will she have to wait for the jury verdict to learn the outcome of her case, or can she ask the prosecutor to call her?

Jessica won't have to wait. Almost every state with a victim's right act provides that the victim has the right to be informed of the final disposition of his or her case. The final disposition could be a jury verdict, as in Jessica's case, or the offender's acquittal or conviction after a bench trial, the dismissal of charges prior to prosecution, or a plea bargain. Any victim who wants notice of the final disposition should inform the prosecutor, and be sure that the prosecutor has his or her current address and telephone number.

Going to Court in Your State

ALABAMA

Witness Fees: Witnesses are entitled to 15¢ per mile and $15 per day.

ALASKA

Witness Fees: Witnesses who travel from outside the state of Alaska must be tendered round trip air fare, reasonable incidental expenses and $20 per day.

Employment: If an employer fires or disciplines an employee for missing work to cooperate with the criminal justice process the victim may sue the employer to recover his or her actual damages plus punitive damages of three times the actual damages.

ARIZONA

Witness Fees: Indigent witnesses who travel from within the state of Arizona are allowed their reasonable expenses, if they travel from another county. Witnesses who travel from outside the state of Arizona must be tendered 10¢ per mile and $5 per day.

ARKANSAS

Witness fees: Witnesses are entitled to 5¢ per mile (if they come from another county) and $5 per day. Witnesses who travel from outside the state of Arkansas must be tendered 12¢ per mile, $25 per day and travel, lodging and meal expenses.

Employment: Prosecutors should intercede with employers on behalf of victims to minimize loss of wages or benefits.

CALIFORNIA

Witness Fees: Witnesses are entitled to $12 per day (or $18 a day if their court appearance results in lost wages) plus reasonable expenses. Witnesses who travel from outside the state of California must be tendered 10¢ per mile (or airfare and 20¢ per mile to and from the airport) and $20 per day.

COLORADO

Witness Fees: Witnesses are entitled to 15¢ per mile and from $1.50 to $2.50 per day. Witnesses who travel from outside the state of Colorado must be tendered 10¢ per mile, or roundtrip airfare and $20 per day.

Employment: Prosecutors should intercede with employers on behalf of victims to minimize loss of wages or benefits.

It is illegal to discharge or discipline an employee who is a victim for honoring a subpoena or participating in the preparation of the prosecution.

CONNECTICUT

Witness Fees: Witnesses are entitled to 10¢ per mile and 50¢ per day. Witnesses who travel from outside the state of Connecticut must be tendered 10¢ per mile and $5 per day.

Employment: The victim cannot be fired, harassed or retaliated against by an employer for appearing under a subpoena as a witness.

DELAWARE

*Witness Fees:*Witnesses are entitled to 3¢ per mile and $2 per day. Witnesses who travel from outside the state must be tendered 10¢ per mile and $5 per day.

Employment: Prosecutors should intercede with employers on behalf of victims to minimize loss of wages or benefits.

DISTRICT OF COLUMBIA

*Witness Fees:*Witnesses are entitled to 25¢ per mile and $40 per day. Witnesses who travel from outside the District must be tendered the same amount as witnesses in U.S. District Courts.

FLORIDA

Witness Fees: Witnesses are entitled to 6¢ per mile and $5 per day. Witnesses who travel from outside the state of Florida must be tendered 10¢ per mile and $5 per day.

Employment: It is illegal to terminate any person who is absent from work because he or she is obeying a subpoena. If wrongfully discharged, the employee may sue for his or her actual damages, attorney fees and for punitive damages. Prosecutors should intercede with employers on behalf of victims to minimize loss of wages or benefits.

GEORGIA

Witness Fees: Witnesses are entitled to 20¢ per mile and $10 per day. Witnesses who travel from outside the state of Georgia must be tendered 12¢ per mile and $25 per day.

HAWAII

Witness Fees: Witnesses from the same island are entitled to reasonable mileage and $20 per day. In state witnesses who travel from another island are allowed their reasonable airfare and $55 per day. Witnesses who travel from another state must be tendered their reasonable airfare and $110 per day.

Employment: It is illegal for an employer to fire an employee who misses work to obey a subpoena. A fired employee may bring an action against the employer for reinstatement, attorney fees and up to six weeks of lost wages.

IDAHO

Witness Fees: Witnesses are entitled to $8 per day plus the reasonable costs of lodging. Witnesses who travel from outside the state must be tendered 15¢ per mile and $5 per day.

ILLINOIS

Witness Fees:Witnesses are entitled to 20¢ per mile and $20 per day.

Employment: Prosecutors should intercede with employers on behalf of victims to minimize loss of wages or benefits.

INDIANA

Witness Fees: Witnesses are entitled to mileage at the same rate paid to state officials and $5 per day. Witnesses who travel from outside the state of Indiana must be tendered mileage at the same rate paid to state officials and $15 per day.

Employment : It is a Class B misdemeanor to dismiss or deprive an employee of benefits because he or she responds to a criminal court subpoena.

IOWA

Witness Fees: Witnesses are entitled to $10 per full day. Mileage is set by local governing bodies and may not exceed the amount allowed by IRS rules.

Employment: It is a misdemeanor for an employer to fire or demote a witness who misses work because he or she attends court in response to a subpoena. The employee may recover actual damages, court costs and attorney fees.

KANSAS

Witness Fees: Witnesses are entitled to mileage at the rate fixed annually by the Secretary of Administration and $10 per day plus the costs of food and lodging. Witnesses who travel from outside the state must be tendered the same mileage and per diem as those who travel within the state.

KENTUCKY

Witness Fees: Witnesses are entitled to mileage at a rate fixed by the Secretary of the Finance and Administration Cabinet. Witnesses who travel from outside the state of Kentucky must be tendered 10¢ per mile and $5 per day.

Employment: Prosecutors should intercede with employers on behalf of victims to minimize loss of wages or benefits.

LOUISIANA

Witness Fees: Witnesses are entitled to 5¢ per mile and $3 per day. Witnesses who travel from outside the state of Louisiana must be tendered 10¢ per mile and $5 per day.

Employment: Prosecutors should intercede with employers on behalf of victims to minimize loss of wages or benefits.

MAINE

Witness Fees: Witnesses are entitled to 22¢ per mile and $10 per day. Witnesses who travel from outside the state of Maine must be tendered 10¢ per mile and $15 per day, plus a reasonable allowance for meals and lodging.

MARYLAND

Witness Fees: Witnesses are entitled to from 4¢ to 12¢ per mile, and from $1 to $5 per day, depending on the county. Witnesses who travel from outside the state of Maryland must be tendered 10¢ per mile and $5 per day.

Employment: It is illegal for an employer to fire a worker who misses work in order to obey a subpoena. Employers who break this law are subject to a fine of up to $1,000. Prosecutors should intercede with employers on behalf of victims to minimize loss of wages or benefits.

MASSACHUSETTS

Witness Fees: Witnesses are entitled to 10¢ per mile and $6 per day. Witnesses who travel from outside the state of Massachusetts must be tendered 10¢ per mile and $5 per day.

Employment: It is illegal to fire a victim or witness who misses work due to a subpoena, if the employee gives his or her employer prior notice of the required court attendance. An employer who fires such an employee is subject to a $200 fine and imprisonment of up to one month. Prosecutors should intercede with employers on behalf of victims to minimize loss of wages or benefits.

MICHIGAN

Witness Fees: Witnesses are entitled to 10¢ per mile and $12 per day (or $15 per day if the witness misses work.)

Employment: It is a misdemeanor, and punishable as contempt of court, for an employer to fire or discipline, or threaten to fire or discipline a victim who attends court pursuant to a subpoena or pursuant to the prosecutor's request.

MINNESOTA

Witness Fees: Witnesses are entitled to 24¢ per mile and $10 per day, as well as up to $40 per day in reasonable expenses. Witnesses who travel from outside the state of Minnesota must be tendered 10¢ per mile and $5 per day.

Employment: It is a misdemeanor for an employer to fire or discipline or threaten to fire or discipline an employee who misses work due to a subpoena. The employer may also be punished for contempt of court. The court shall order the employer to offer the fired worker reinstatement.

MISSOURI

Witness Fees: Witnesses who attend court in their county of residence are entitled to $3 per day. Witnesses who attend court in a different county are entitled to 7¢ per mile and $4 per day. Witnesses who travel from outside the state of Missouri must be tendered 10¢ per mile and $15 per day.

Employment: Prosecutors should intercede with employers on behalf of victims to minimize loss of wages or benefits.

MISSISSIPPI

Witness Fees: Witnesses are entitled to 5¢ per mile and $1.50 per day. Witnesses who travel from outside the state of Mississippi must be tendered 10¢ per mile and $5 per day.

MONTANA

Witness Fees: Witnesses are entitled to 3¢ less per mile than the rate set by the IRS and $10 per day. Witnesses from outside the state must be tendered the same mileage allowance and the reasonable cost of meals and lodging, not to exceed $23.50 for meals and $50 for lodging.

Employment: Prosecutors should intercede with employers on behalf of victims to minimize loss of wages or benefits.

NEBRASKA

Witness Fees: Witnesses are entitled to 24¢ per mile and $20 per day. Witnesses who travel from outside the state of Nebraska must be tendered 24¢ per mile and $5 per day.

Employment: Prosecutors should intercede with employers on behalf of victims to minimize loss of wages or benefits.

NEVADA

Witness Fees: Witnesses are entitled to 19¢ per mile and $25 per day. Witnesses who travel from outside the state of Nevada must be tendered the same amount.

Employment: It is a misdemeanor for an employer to fire a worker who misses work in order to obey a subpoena. A fired employee may sue for his or her lost wages and benefits, reinstatement in the job, and attorney fees.

NEW HAMPSHIRE

Witness Fees: Witnesses are entitled to 17¢ per mile and $12 per day. Witnesses who travel from outside the state of New Hampshire must be tendered 10¢ per mile and $5 per day.

NEW JERSEY

Witness Fees: Witnesses who attend court in the county of their residence are entitled to $2 per day. Witnesses who attend court in another county are entitled to $2 for every 30 miles traveled and $2 per day. Witnesses who travel from outside the state of New Jersey must be tendered 10¢ per mile and $5 per day.

Employment: The prosecutor should notify the employer if co-operation will cause the employee to be absent from work.

NEW MEXICO

Witness Fees: Witnesses are entitled to 25¢ per mile and up to $75 per day, or the actual cost of lodging plus $22.50 for meals. Witnesses who travel from outside the state of New Mexico must be tendered 5¢ per mile and $2 per day.

Employment: The prosecutor must notify the employer of the necessity of the victim's cooperation and testimony and that it may require his or her absence from work.

NEW YORK

Witness Fees: Witnesses are entitled to 23¢ per mile and $15 per day. Witnesses who travel from outside the state of New York must be tendered 10¢ per mile and $5 per day.

Employment: Prosecutors should intercede with employers on behalf of victims to minimize loss of wages or benefits.

NORTH CAROLINA

Witness Fees: Witnesses are entitled to mileage at the rate paid state employees and $5 per day. Witnesses who travel from outside the state of North Carolina must be tendered 10¢ per mile and $5 per day.

Employment: Prosecutors should intercede with employers on behalf of victims to minimize loss of wages or benefits.

NORTH DAKOTA

Witness Fees: Witnesses are entitled to 20¢ per mile and $25 per day. Witnesses who travel from outside the state of North Dakota must be tendered the same amount.

Employment: Prosecutors should intercede with employers on behalf of victims to minimize loss of wages or benefits.

OHIO

Witness Fees: Witnesses are entitled to 10¢ per mile and $12 per whole day, $6 per half day. Witnesses who travel from outside the state of Ohio must be tendered 10¢ per mile and $5 per day.

Employment: The victim has the right to attend court without being discharged, losing pay or being otherwise penalized.

OKLAHOMA

Witness Fees: Witnesses who travel less than 60 miles are entitled to $5 per day and 15¢ per mile. Witnesses who travel more than 60 miles are allowed $12 per day and 15¢ per mile. Witnesses who travel from outside the state of Oklahoma must be tendered 10¢ per mile and $5 per day.

Employment: Prosecutors should intercede with employers on behalf of victims to minimize loss of wages or benefits.

OREGON

Witness Fees: Witnesses are entitled to 8¢ per mile and $5 per day. Witnesses who travel from outside the state of Oregon must be tendered 10¢ per mile and $5 per day.

PENNSYLVANIA

Witness Fees: Witnesses are entitled to 7¢ per mile and $5 per day plus lodging if the witness is required to stay longer than one day and if the witness has traveled more than 50 miles. Witnesses who travel from outside the state of Pennsylvania must be tendered 10¢ per mile and $5 per day.

Employment: It is illegal to fire or withhold benefits from an employee who attends court because he or she was a victim of, or witness to a crime. An employee who is wrongfully fired or penalized may bring a civil action and recover lost wages and benefits, may be reinstated and may recover his or her attorney fees.

RHODE ISLAND

Witness Fees: Witnesses are entitled to 10¢ per mile and $10 per day. Witnesses who travel from outside the state of Rhode Island must be tendered 10¢ per mile and $5 per day.

Employment: Prosecutors should intercede with employers on behalf of victims to minimize loss of wages or benefits.

SOUTH CAROLINA

Witness Fees: Witnesses are entitled to a reasonable witness fee and compensation for their out of pocket expenses. Witnesses who travel from outside the state of South Carolina must be tendered 10¢ per mile and $5 per day.

Employment: Prosecutors should intercede with employers on behalf of victims to minimize loss of wages or benefits.

SOUTH DAKOTA

Witness Fees: Witnesses are entitled to 21¢ per mile and $20 per day.

TENNESSEE

Witness Fees: Witnesses are entitled to 4¢ per mile and $1 per day. Witnesses who travel from another county are entitled to $40 per day. Witnesses who travel from outside the state of Tennessee must be tendered the same amount that witnesses who travel from another county receive.

TEXAS

Witness Fees: Witnesses are entitled to 6¢ per mile and $1.50 per day. Witnesses who travel from another county are entitled to up to 16¢ per mile and $50 per day. Witnesses who travel from outside the state of Texas must be tendered an amount not in excess of 16¢ per mile and $50 per day living expenses.

Employment: Prosecutors should intercede with employers on behalf of victims to minimize loss of wages or benefits.

UTAH

Witness Fees: Witnesses are entitled to 25¢ per mile after traveling 50 miles and $17 per day. Witnesses who travel from outside the state of Utah must be tendered not more than 20¢ per mile and $30 per day.

Employment: Prosecutors should intercede with employers on behalf of victims to minimize loss of wages or benefits.

VERMONT

Witness Fees: Witnesses are entitled to 8¢ per mile and $10 per day. Witnesses who travel from outside the state of Vermont must be tendered 10¢ per mile and $10 per day.

Employment: The prosecutor should provide employer intercession services.

VIRGINIA

Witness Fees: Witnesses are entitled to reasonable mileage and tolls. Witnesses who travel from outside the state of Virginia must be tendered a reasonable amount.

Employment: The prosecutor should provide employer intercession services.

WASHINGTON

Witness Fees: Witnesses are entitled to mileage as established periodically by the director of financial management and from $10 to $25 per day. Witnesses who travel from outside the state of Washington must be tendered 10¢ per mile and $5 per day.

Employment: Prosecutors should intercede with employers on behalf of victims to minimize loss of wages or benefits.

WEST VIRGINIA

Witness Fees: Witnesses are entitled to 15¢ per mile and from $10 to $20 per day. Witnesses who travel from outside the state of West Virginia must be tendered 10¢ per mile and $5 per day.

Employment: Prosecutors should intercede with employers on behalf of victims to minimize loss of wages or benefits.

WISCONSIN

Witness Fees: Witnesses are entitled to 20¢ per mile and $16 per day. Witnesses who travel from outside the state of Wisconsin must be tendered 10¢ per mile and $5 per day.

Employment: Prosecutors should intercede with employers on behalf of victims to minimize loss of wages or benefits.

WYOMING

Witness Fees: Witnesses are entitled to 23¢ per mile and $10 per day.

Employment: A victim or witness who misses work in order to obey a subpoena shall not suffer any change in terms of employment solely due to complying with the subpoena.

CHAPTER 3

THE VICTIM'S RIGHT
TO PARTICIPATION IN SENTENCING

On a sunny afternoon in April, Rochelle stopped for gas at a convenience store. She was between sales calls and decided to get a cold drink before her next appointment. She was filling her cup when suddenly a man in the store began shouting. She turned and saw that a bearded man wearing a baseball cap was pointing a handgun at the cashier. Rochelle and the other customers in the store lay face down on the floor as the robber directed, while the cashier filled a bag with money.

Rochelle had her eyes shut tightly. She heard the robber's footsteps coming toward her, and then he was shouting again. She didn't realize that he was shouting at her to get up. Then he kicked her in the side and she scrambled to her feet. Holding Rochelle before him as a shield, the robber pushed her out of the store and into his car.

Although it seemed like hours, within minutes several squad cars were following the robber and Rochelle, his hostage. The police had anticipated that he would head for the interstate, and when he drove onto an entrance ramp, he found his path blocked. The robber swerved into a ditch, and then pulled Rochelle out of the car, again using her as a shield.

The robber demanded that the police officers at the barricade move aside. He was walking backwards, pulling her with him towards one of their cars, when he stumbled and fell. Rochelle immediately dove forward onto the ground; she heard several gunshots explode near her. She didn't move until a police officer knelt beside her and asked her if she were hurt. Her captor was lying on his stomach and a police officer was frisking him. Rochelle saw him sit up, bleeding from a wound in his shoulder.

Rochelle returned to work in three days, but two weeks later she suffered a complete breakdown and spent 30 days in a psychiatric unit for post traumatic stress disorder. After her discharge from the hospital, she found that she could not enter a convenience store. She has recurring nightmares, when she is able to sleep. Her assailant was convicted of charges of armed robbery and kidnapping. He has not yet been sentenced.

Rochelle testified at the trial and was present when the jury returned with a verdict of guilty on both counts. Instead of sentencing the defendant, the judge ordered a presentence investigation, and announced that the sentencing hearing would be in one month. What is the purpose of this?

Most state laws require in the case of serious crimes (such as felonies or misdemeanors that result in the death of, or serious injury to, another person) that a presentence investigation be conducted. The presentence investigation is usually carried out by a probation officer or other court services officer. This officer is charged with providing information to the court on a number of issues. Those issues include:

- The nature of the crime itself
- The identity of the defendant
- The defendant's prior criminal record, education, family and social circumstances
- The need for and likelihood of rehabilitation
- A sentencing recommendation
- Information concerning the victim and the impact that the crime had on the victim

Rochelle has not yet met with the probation officer who was assigned to prepare the presentence report, but she spoke with her briefly on the telephone. She told Rochelle that she would have the opportunity to prepare a victim impact statement for the presentence report. What sort of information should Rochelle gather and be prepared to give the officer?

A typical victim impact statement includes the following information:

1. The identity of the victim or victims of the offense.
2. An itemization of the economic loss suffered by the victim.

3. Information regarding compensation (if any) that the victim has received, such as insurance proceeds or restitution from the offender.
4. A description of any physical injury suffered by the victim, including information on its severity and whether or not the injury is permanent in nature.
5. A description of the crime's effects on the victim's personal welfare and the impact of the offense on the victim's personal, family and business relationships.
6. Details regarding any requests for psychological services from the victim or the victim's family.
7. Identification of any other needs for services, such as medical or rehabilitation services.
8. The victim's recommendations for sentencing.
9. Information regarding any other significant impact the crime had on the victim.

New Jersey law requires that, in addition to the foregoing information, the statement include "...an assessment of the gravity and seriousness of harm inflicted on the victim, including whether or not the defendant knew or reasonably should have known that the victim of the offense was particularly vulnerable or incapable of resistance due to advanced age, disability, ill-health or extreme youth, or was for any other reason substantially incapable of exercising normal physical or mental power of resistance."

An extremely important part of the victim impact statement is a description of the economic consequences of the crime. When assessing your loss, consider the following:

- Hospital and medical bills
- Counseling fees
- Damage to or loss of property
- Lost wages and loss of future earnings
- Permanent disability
- Rehabilitative costs
- Cost of glasses, crutches, hearing aids, artificial limbs and other devices
- Funeral expenses

Rochelle wants the judge to know how this crime has affected her, but she has days when it is too painful for her to think about it. Does she have to give a victim impact statement if she doesn't want to?

No. Neither the court nor the investigator can legally require or force Rochelle to give a statement or cooperate with the presentence investigation. However, Rochelle should seriously consider submitting such a statement. Through the victim impact statement, Rochelle can make her feelings and recommendations known to the court, without having to appear in person again, and without having to answer questions from defendant's lawyer.

The statement is typically included in the presentence report, or filed with the case file for the judge's review if there is no presentence report ordered. This is a departure from usual court procedure, because under the rules of evidence such a statement is hearsay, and in most cases hearsay is not admissible in court. Normally, any person wishing to communicate with the court regarding the case would have to do so in the courtroom, on the witness stand, where he or she would be subject to cross examination.

The victim impact statement is a more convenient and less stressful way to communicate with the court. Another benefit is that the statement may contain information that would help the court make an appropriate restitution order.

Many states have laws that require that a victim impact statement be prepared as a part of the presentence investigation. This does not create a legal responsibility for the victim to cooperate. It mandates, instead, that the investigator attempt to contact the victim and obtain the victim's input. The investigator should try to provide the court with an assessment of the impact of the crime on the victim, even if the victim does not wish to participate in the process.

Rochelle would like to know what sentencing recommendation the probation officer is going to make. Can she read the presentence report before it is filed with the court?

Probably not. In all states, the presentence report is considered a confidential document, and under most state laws only the judge, the prosecutor and the defendant's attorney are allowed to read it. In fact, in many states, even the defendant may not see the report, although his or her attorney may discuss its contents with him. However, there are a few states that make exceptions to this rule:

Alaska: The victim has the right to see the portions of the presentence report that contain the summary or description of the crime, the defendant's version of the crime, the victim's statement and the sentencing recommendation.

Arizona: The victim has the right to read the presentence report, if it is available to the defendant.

California: The victim has the right to review the sentence recommendation portion of the presentence investigation.

Colorado: The victim has the right to view both the presentence report and the victim impact statement.

New York: The victim has the right to view the victim impact section of the presentence report.

Rochelle wants her abductor to receive the harshest sentence possible under the law. She would like to speak with the judge personally, to stress to him how the crime has affected her life. May she see the judge in his office and urge him to sentence the defendant to the longest prison term possible?

No. It would improper for the judge to meet privately with Rochelle to discuss the case. However, almost all states have laws that grant the victims of serious crimes the right to be present at the sentencing hearing, and to address the court in person regarding the crime. Some states give the victim the option of either making a sworn statement (a statement given under oath from the witness stand, during which the victim must answer questions put to him or her by the prosecutor and the defense) or simply addressing the court. Many states allow the victim to personally present a written statement, in lieu of an oral statement.

In a few states, crime victims may take advantage of modern video technology. In Arizona, the victim has the option to submit any victim impact statement orally, in written form, or by submitting a videotape for the court to view. In California, the victim is entitled to appear at the sentencing hearing and express his or her views, and may do so by means of an audiotape or videotape. A victim who submits an audio or videotape avoids the stress of a court appearance, but makes a more personal impression than that left by a written statement.

What if Rochelle suffers a relapse of her stress-related mental disorder and is not able to prepare a victim impact statement or appear at the sentencing?

All states that encourage victim participation in sentencing also make allowance for victims who are unable to speak for themselves. The victim of a homicide obviously cannot make a victim impact statement. Neither can a young child who has been the victim of a crime, or a person who is mentally or physically disabled. For this reason, most state laws allow the victim's parents, or spouse, or guardian or next of kin, or other appropriate representative to speak for the victim, if he or she cannot do so.

A Note about "Truth in Sentencing"

News articles or reports about parolees or ex cons who commit new crimes frequently state that the offender had only served a portion of the sentence originally imposed. People who hear these stories are often confused about why an inmate who received a long sentence for a crime was out and committing new crimes when he should have still been doing time.

Many sentences are reduced by "good time" credits, and convicts may be eligible for release after serving only a small portion of their sentences. In a few states, new laws known as "truth in sentencing laws," are aimed at addressing the public's right to know what a sentence really means.

In California, for example, the law requires that the court inform the victim that ⅓ to ½ of the defendant's sentence may be reduced by good time credits. And Illinois law requires that at the time of sentencing, the court inform the victim of the minimum amount of time that the defendant may actually be imprisoned, considering good conduct credit.

State by State Guide to
Victim Participation in Sentencing

ALABAMA

If a presentence investigation is ordered, the report may contain a victim impact statement.

ALASKA

In felony cases, the presentence report should contain a victim impact statement.

The victim has the right to the address and telephone number of the officer preparing the presentence report.

The victim has the right to see the portions of the presentence report that contain the summary or description of the crime, the defendant's version of the crime, the victim's statement and the sentencing recommendation.

The victim of a felony or domestic violence has the right to appear personally before the court at the sentencing hearing and make a sworn or unsworn statement, or submit a written statement relevant to sentencing. The statement may contain information regarding the extent of harm to the victim, the need for restitution and the victim's recommendation for sentencing.

ARIZONA

The prosecutor shall inform the victim that he or she has the right to make a victim impact statement. The prosecutor shall inform the victim of the function of the presentence report, and give the victim the name and number of the person preparing the report.

The victim impact statement may be made orally to the individual preparing the presentence report, or may be submitted in writing.

The victim has the right to read the presentence report if it is available to the defendant.

The victim has the right to appear personally before the court at the sentencing hearing and make a statement.

ARKANSAS

The victim has the right to appear personally before the court at the sentencing hearing and make a statement.

CALIFORNIA

In the case of felony convictions, the presentence report must contain a victim impact statement.

The victim has the right to review the sentence recommendation portion of the presentence investigation.

The victim has the right to appear personally before the court at the sentencing hearing and make a statement.

COLORADO

If a presentence investigation is ordered, the report must contain a victim impact statement. If no investigation is ordered, a separate victim impact statement must be prepared.

The prosecutor shall provide the victim with the name and telephone number of the probation officer who is preparing the pre-sentence report, and inform the victim that he or she has the right to make a victim impact statement.

The victim has the right to view both the presentence report and the victim impact statement.

The victim has the right to appear personally before the court at the sentencing hearing and present a written victim impact statement or make an oral statement to the court regarding the harm that he or she has sustained due to the crime.

CONNECTICUT

The victim has the right to submit a statement to the prosecutor regarding the extent of his or her injuries, financial losses and loss of earnings resulting from the crime, prior to the imposition of sentence.

The victim has the right to appear personally before the court at the sentencing hearing and make a statement. The victim has the option of submitting a written statement.

DELAWARE

A victim impact statement must be prepared and presented to the court with the presentence report in all felony cases, and in misdemeanors that resulted in physical injury or death.

If a presentence report is not required, the victim has the right to appear personally before the court at the sentencing hearing and present an impact statement.

DISTRICT OF COLUMBIA

The victim of a crime of violence has the right to submit a victim impact statement to the court prior to the imposition of sentence.

FLORIDA

If a presentence investigation is ordered, the report shall contain information regarding the extent of the victim's loss.

The victim has the right to appear personally at sentencing and make a statement under oath. The victim also has the option of making a written statement regarding the facts of the case and the impact of the crime on him or her.

The victim of a felony has the right to be consulted by the prosecutor regarding his or her views on the sentencing of the offender.

GEORGIA

The victim has the right to prepare a victim impact statement that is attached to the case file for the court's review. The victim has the right to appear personally before the court at the sentencing hearing and make a statement regarding the crime and the offender.

HAWAII

If a presentence investigation is ordered, the report must contain information from the victim regarding the impact of the crime.

IDAHO

If a presentence investigation is ordered, the report must contain a statement regarding the victim's economic loss. The presentence investigator should consult with the victim regarding the impact that the crime has had upon his or her life.

The victim has the right to appear personally before the court at the sentencing hearing and address the court, under oath.

ILLINOIS

The victim of a violent crime, or a drunk driving offense, may submit a written statement regarding the impact of the crime and offer evidence in aggravation or mitigation.

The victim has the right to address the court at sentencing regarding the impact of the crime. The statement must be in writing, and it must be prepared ahead of time, in cooperation with the prosecutor's office.

INDIANA

The victim has the right to submit a victim impact statement for the presentence investigation.

The victim has the right to seven days notice of the sentencing hearing, at which he or she may make an oral statement or present a written statement.

IOWA

If a presentence investigation is ordered, the report shall contain information regarding the extent of harm suffered by the victim.

The victim has the right to file a victim impact statement with the prosecutor, and that statement shall be included in the presentence investigation report. If no report is prepared, the victim impact statement is to be submitted to the judge prior to sentencing.

KANSAS

If a presentence investigation is ordered, it must contain information from the victim, including the financial, social, physical and psychological harm caused by the offender, and the need for restitution. When appropriate, the views and the concerns of the victim should be brought to the attention of the court.

The victim has the right to appear personally before the court at sentencing, and to be heard, to the extent that it does not interfere with the constitutional rights of the defendant.

KENTUCKY

The victim has the right to submit a written victim impact statement to the probation officer for inclusion in the presentence report, or to be presented to the court if no presentence report is ordered.

LOUISIANA

The victim has the right to present a victim impact statement orally or in writing to be filed with the court.

The victim has the right to appear personally before the court at the sentencing hearing and to be heard.

The victim has the right to consult with the prosecutor regarding sentencing and the use of sentencing alternatives.

MAINE

The victim has the right to appear personally before the court at the sentencing hearing or the victim may submit a written statement, which becomes part of the official court record.

MARYLAND

In the case of crimes causing personal or other serious injury, if a presentence report is ordered, it should contain a victim impact statement. If no presentence report is ordered, a victim impact statement may be submitted directly to the court.

At the judge's discretion, the victim of the crime may address the court, under oath, at sentencing.

MASSACHUSETTS

If a presentence report is ordered, it must contain a victim impact statement.

The victim has the right to appear personally before the court at the sentencing hearing and make an oral statement at the hearing or submit a written statement to the court.

MICHIGAN

If a presentence investigation is ordered, the report must include a victim impact statement, the victim may submit the statement orally or in writing.

The victim has the right to appear personally before the court at the sentencing hearing and make a statement regarding the harm or trauma suffered by the victim, the extent of property or economic loss, the need for restitution and the victim's recommendation regarding sentencing.

MINNESOTA

If a presentence investigation is ordered the report must include information regarding the circumstances of the offense and the harm that it caused others, including information regarding the victim. The investigator must make a good faith effort to contact the victim.

The victim is entitled to notice of the court's sentencing options.

The victim may present an impact statement to the court in person or in writing, regarding the harm or trauma to the victim, the victim's economic loss and the victim's views on the proposed disposition of the case. At the victim's request, the prosecutor shall present the statement orally to the court.

MISSISSIPPI

If a presentence investigation is ordered, a victim impact statement must be included in the presentence report. If there is no presentence report, the victim may submit a written statement to the prosecutor, who will present it to the judge before sentencing.

The victim has the right to be present at the sentencing hearing and may make an oral statement with the judge's permission.

MISSOURI

The victim has the right to appear personally, or through counsel, before the court at the sentencing hearing or to submit a written statement to the court regarding the seriousness of the crime and the loss and/or injury to the victim and the need for restitution.

MONTANA

If a presentence investigation is ordered, the report must contain information regarding the harm to the victim, the victim's family, the community and any pecuniary loss.

NEBRASKA

The victim has the right to prompt notice of the sentencing hearing.

NEVADA

If a presentence investigation is ordered, the report must contain information regarding the effect of the crime on the victim.

The victim has the right to appear personally, or through counsel, before the court at the sentencing hearing to express his or her views regarding the crime, the offender, and the need for restitution.

NEW HAMPSHIRE

The victim has the right to have input in the presentence report.

The victim of a violent crime has the right to appear personally or through counsel at sentencing and address the court regarding the crime, the offender and the need for restitution. The victim may address the court orally or in writing.

NEW JERSEY

If a presentence investigation is ordered, the report should contain a statement from the victim.

The victim has the right to appear personally before the court at the sentencing hearing and make a statement prior to sentencing.

NEW MEXICO

The victim has the right to submit a victim impact statement to the court, and to have assistance in executing a written statement.

The victim has the right to appear personally before the court at the sentencing hearing and to be heard prior to the pronouncement of the sentence.

NEW YORK

If a presentence investigation is ordered, the report should contain a victim impact statement, unless it would be of no relevance to the disposition of the case.

The victim has the right to view the victim impact portion of the presentence report.

The victim has the right to appear personally before the court at the sentencing hearing and make a statement. The court must consider the victim's views when imposing sentence.

NORTH CAROLINA

The victim has the right to have a victim impact statement prepared for consideration by the court.

The victim has the right to appear personally before the court at the sentencing hearing.

NORTH DAKOTA

If a presentence investigation is ordered, it should contain a victim impact statement. If no investigation is ordered, the victim may submit a written statement to the prosecutor, to be submitted to the sentencing court.

The victim of a violent crime may appear personally at the sentencing hearing and make a statement under oath, subject to the court's approval.

OHIO

A victim impact statement must be prepared in felony cases.

The victim of violent crime has the right to make a statement to the court regarding sentencing, subject to any reasonable terms set by the court. The court may require that the statement be made orally, or in writing.

OKLAHOMA

If a presentence investigation is ordered, the report should contain a victim impact statement.

The victim has the right to present the court with a written victim impact statement or appear personally at the sentencing hearing and give an oral statement.

OREGON

If a presentence investigation is ordered, the report should include a statement from the victim.

The victim has the right to appear personally before the court at the sentencing hearing or to appear by counsel, and make a statement regarding the crime, the offender, the impact of the crime and the need for restitution.

PENNSYLVANIA

If a presentence investigation is ordered, the report should contain a victim impact statement.

Any victim impact statement that is submitted should be considered by the court prior to sentencing.

RHODE ISLAND

A victim has the right to be consulted during the preparation of the presentence investigation report. The victim has the right to prepare a written victim impact statement to be presented to the court prior to sentencing.

A victim has the right to appear personally before the court at the sentencing hearing and make a statement regarding the impact of the crime. This statement is to be presented before the attorneys present their recommendations for sentencing and before the court imposes sentence.

SOUTH CAROLINA

The victim has the right to submit a written statement to the court regarding the crime and the offender. In the alternative, the victim may appear personally before the court at the sentencing hearing and make an oral statement. The victim is entitled to the assistance of the solicitor's office in preparing the statement.

SOUTH DAKOTA

The victim has the right to appear personally before the court at the sentencing hearing and address the court regarding the impact of the crime and may comment on the sentence that may be imposed. In the alternative, the victim may submit a written statement.

TENNESSEE

All presentence investigation reports prepared for felony offenses should contain a victim impact statement. The sentencing judge shall consider the victim impact statement prior to sentencing.

The victim of a violent crime has the right to appear personally before the court at the sentencing hearing and make a statement.

TEXAS

The victim has the right to provide information to be included in a presentence investigation report regarding the impact of the crime by oral testimony or by a written statement. This statement shall be considered by the court prior to the imposition of sentence.

The victim has the right to appear personally before the court at the sentencing hearing and present a statement regarding his or her views of the offense, the offender and the impact of the crime. The statement is to be made after the sentence is pronounced.

UTAH

The state of Utah has no special provisions regarding the preparation of victim impact statements for inclusion in presentence investigation reports, or for victim participation during the sentencing hearing.

VERMONT

The victim has the right to appear personally before the court at the sentencing hearing and express his or her views regarding the offense, the offender and the need for restitution.

VIRGINIA

The presentence investigation report for violent crimes should contain a victim impact statement. If no presentence investigation is ordered, the prosecutor may prepare a victim impact statement for the court's consideration.

WASHINGTON

The victim has the right to submit a victim impact statement to the court and may request the assistance of the prosecutor in preparing the statement.

The victim has the right to appear personally before the court, or to appear through a representative, and present a statement at sentencing.

WEST VIRGINIA

If the court orders a presentence investigation, the report should contain a victim impact statement. If a presentence investigation report is not ordered, the prosecutor may request that a victim impact statement be prepared.

The victim has the right to appear personally before the court at the sentencing hearing and make a statement regarding the facts of the case and the victim's losses, prior to the imposition of the sentence. The victim may choose to submit a written statement to be filed with the court instead.

WISCONSIN

If a presentence investigation is ordered, the report should contain information regarding the impact of the crime on the victim. The court should consider this information in imposing sentence.

WYOMING

The victim has the right to the name and telephone number of the person preparing the presentence investigation report. The victim has the right to give an oral statement for inclusion in the report or may submit the impact statement in writing.

The victim has the right to appear personally before the court at the sentencing hearing and make a statement prior to the imposition of the sentence.

CHAPTER 4

POST CONVICTION HEARINGS

Your Right to Notice and Participation

Robert's daughter was brutally murdered by her estranged boyfriend. Although he was initially charged with first degree murder, the killer entered into a plea bargain, and the first degree murder charge was reduced to a charge of murder in the second degree. Robert was relieved that his daughter's killer received the maximum sentence allowed in his state for second degree murder, a term of 30 years. However, under state law the killer will be eligible for parole after serving only seven years of his sentence. Robert has vowed to do everything he can to see that the man who killed his daughter remains behind bars.

Robert's state gives crime victims the right to notice of post conviction hearings, such as parole hearings, but Robert wasn't really the victim of this crime. Does he have any rights?

Yes. Most states provide the victims of violent crime with notice regarding post-conviction hearings. In the states that make such provision, there are laws that allow participation by victim representatives. Under these laws, in the event that the victim is unable to assert his or her rights, the victim's family, or the court may designate a representative to receive notice and participate in the same manner as the victim would if he or she were able.

The law recognizes many reasons why the victim might not be able to exercise those rights. For example, if the victim is a child, is not mentally competent, is physically disabled or ill, or as in the case of Robert's daughter, is dead, a representative may take the victim's place.

Although the killer pleaded guilty, the defense attorney stated that they might appeal the sentence imposed. What are Robert's rights in the event an appeal is filed?

Some state laws provide that the victim of a violent crime is entitled to notice if the offender appeals, and reports regarding the status of the appeal, and the result of the appeal. In a state without a law that addresses victim's rights during the appeals process, the victim should call the prosecutor handling the appeal to learn the status of the case, since information regarding the appeal is a matter of public record.

Michigan law provides a model for the rights of crime victims in the event the offender appeals his conviction or sentence. That law states that the victim has the right to:

> •notice if the offender appeals his or her conviction
> •an explanation of the appeals process
> •notice as to whether the offender will be released on bail during the appeal period
> •notification of the time and place of any appellate court proceedings
> •notice of the result of the appeal.

How will Robert know if the killer is being considered for parole? What can he do about it?

Most states require that before the parole board holds a hearing, it must provide notice to the victim of the crime, or to the victim's representative. However, states usually condition this requirement on the victim's request. This means that the victim must notify the proper authorities of his or her desire to receive notice of parole hearings, and then keep a current mailing address on file with the authorities.

When the victim receives notice of the hearing, he or she will be advised of his or her rights to have input on the decision. Most states allow the victim or the victim's representative to chose between appearing personally to address the parole board and submitting a written statement. In a few states, the victim or the victim's representative has the right to submit a videotape.

In some states, the right to notice and input at parole hearings is limited to victims of very serious crimes, such as rape, armed robbery and kidnapping. In the case of a homicide, the victim's family or representative would participate.

After the hearing, does Robert have the right to know the results?

Yes. Most states require that the victim receive notice if the offender is to be released on parole. Many states require the board to notify the victim of the board's decision, even if parole isn't granted. The victim is entitled to this notice whether or not he or she participates in the hearing.

Some states require that the board provide additional information, such as the date of release, the geographic location of the release, and any parole terms which affect the victim.

Although parole means freedom for a convict, he or she is still subject to supervision. Once released from parole, however, the criminal no longer has any additional restraints on his or her behavior. For this reason, in some states, if the Board is considering a final discharge from parole, the victim has the right to notice of the hearing, and the right to address the board in person or submit a written statement.

Robert feels that the killer got off too lightly, but he's relieved that he'll be spending at least a few years behind bars. But is there any chance that the sentence could be reduced or modified after the fact?

Yes. In many states, courts may modify sentences within a limited time after the original sentence. Many states require notice to victims of any application by the offender for a reduction or modification of sentence, and allow the victim to appear personally at the hearing, or submit a written statement regarding the application.

Robert is aware that with good time credits, the killer might be considered for release even before he serves his minimum term. Can Robert find out when he might be released?

In some states, upon request, the victim has the right to know the offender's earliest release date. In many states, the victim also has the right to advance warning if the offender is to be released because he or she has served his or her sentence.

Some states even allow notice if the offender's security level is changed, such as when the offender is placed in a halfway house, work release center or community corrections program.

In some states, the victim may request and receive notification of the offender's death. Louisiana law has a unique provision that gives the victim's family the right to know the time and place of the offender's execution, and gives a representative of the family the right to be present for the execution.

Robert led the police to his daughter's killer. He sometimes fears that the killer will escape, and try to take revenge on him. Will he be informed if the killer escapes from custody?

Yes, most states require that the victim be notified as soon as possible if the offender escapes, and many also provide that the victim be notified if and when he or she is recaptured. In Alaska, the victim is to be provided with the most recent available photograph as well.

Robert moved after the murder and doesn't want the killer to know of his whereabouts. His current address is on file with the parole board. Will this information be kept confidential?

Yes. In most cases, laws that require victims to keep a current address on file also provide that the address be kept confidential.

Robert read in the newspaper that the governor was considering several requests for pardons or executive clemency. Could his daughter's killer be among them?

If the killer applies for executive clemency, under the laws in many states, the victim or the victim's representative will receive notice of the application, and have the opportunity to submit comments regarding the application to the governor or to the parole board, depending on which of them is charged with considering clemency applications.

Robert has told the authorities of his desire to be notified of any parole hearings held for the man who killed his daughter. He has been sure to keep them advised of his current address. What if they make a mistake and fail to notify him? If the killer is set free, will Robert have any recourse?

Probably not. Most statutes providing for victim notification do not provide for any remedies in the event the laws are not followed. In fact, many states have laws that specifically provide that their victims' rights enactments do not create a cause of action against any public official or agency responsible for their implementation.

Three notable exceptions are the states of Arizona, Oklahoma, and Tennessee. In Arizona, if the defendant is granted a post-conviction release, such as a release on parole, and the victim was not given notice of the proceeding (after requesting it) the victim has the right to request a hearing to have the release re-examined. Additionally, Arizona law gives the victim the right to sue for damages if his or her rights are violated due to gross negligence on the part of the responsible governmental agency.

In Oklahoma, a victim who does not receive proper notice may apply to have the parole decision voided, while the law in Tennessee provides that if the victim was not notified of the parole hearing, the victim may submit a statement and the board may reconsider its decision in light of the victim's statement.

May Robert contact members of the parole board privately to get their assurance that they will not parole the offender?

Under most state laws, members of the parole board cannot conduct private meetings with interested parties. Maryland law does have a provision that is an exception to this rule. If the offender applies for a remission or commutation of his or her sentence, or applies for a pardon, the victim has the right to request a meeting with a member of the commission charged with reviewing the application. And in Missouri, the victim may meet in person with a member of the parole board, if the board is considering an application from the offender for parole.

What about offenders who are sent to mental hospitals instead of prison, such as those who are found "guilty, but mentally ill" or "not guilty by reason of insanity?" Do the victims of their crimes receive notice of their release.

The laws vary from state to state, but many state laws do provide that victims of the mentally ill are entitled to notice if the offender is released from or escapes from the hospital where he or she is committed.

Protect Your Right to Notice

In most states, the victim or the person acting as the victim's representative must request notice of parole hearings, escape, clemency, or modification applications. To preserve your right to notice, make your request to the proper authorities *in writing*. Additionally, be sure that your current address is on file with the proper authorities. The law varies from state to state, so find out from the prosector handling your case who you should contact. It may be the prosecutor, the State Attorney General, the Department of Corrections, or the Board of Pardons and Paroles.

Notice of Post-Conviction Hearings and Victim's Rights to Participation, State by State

ALABAMA

Alabama law provides that the victims of serious crimes are entitled to 30 days notice of parole, early release or furlough hearings. The victim is entitled to make a statement at the hearing or submit his or her views in writing. Victims are entitled to prompt notice if a pardon or parole is granted.

ALASKA

Alaska law provides that the victim has the right to receive notice if the offender is seeking a modification of his or her sentence. The victim has the right to attend the hearing and give sworn testimony or make an unsworn oral presentation regarding the application.

Victims of serious crimes have the right to 30 days notice of parole hearings. The victim may attend the hearing or submit written comments. The board must inform the victim of the outcome of the hearing, and if the offender is to be released, the board must notify the victim of the expected release date and the geographical area of the release. The same provisions apply for offenders seeking to be furloughed.

The victim has the right to submit written comments regarding applications for clemency.

The victim must be notified if the offender escapes from custody, and the department of corrections must provide the victim the most recent available photograph of the offender.

ARIZONA

Arizona law provides that victims be notified, upon request, of the offender's escape from prison or the offender's death.

The victim is entitled to 15 days notice of any application for furlough, and the victim has the right to be present and to present a written statement at any hearing to consider the application.

The victim has the right to 15 days notice of any parole hearing or any hearing at which the board will consider a complete discharge from parole. The victim has the right to be present and to present a written statement regarding the parole application. The victim has the right to receive notice of the decision.

The victim has the right to be informed of the offender's earliest release date, and has the right to 15 days notice prior to the offender's release.

The victim has the right to notice of any post-conviction proceedings, and any decisions that arise from those proceedings. The victim has the right to notice of any hearing affecting the offender's probation, and the right to know the terms of probation, to the extent those terms affect the victim.

The victim has the right to be informed if the offender is admitted to, released or escapes from a mental health facility.

In any post conviction proceeding at which the victim has the right to appear, the victim has the options of appearing personally, submitting a written statement or submitting an audiotape or videotape.

If the defendant is granted a post-conviction release, and the victim was not notified of the proceeding, the victim has the right to request a hearing to have the release reexamined.

ARKANSAS

Arkansas law provides that the victim is entitled to notice of parole hearings and applications for executive clemency or pardons. The victim may appear in person at such hearings, or submit a written statement.

CALIFORNIA

California law provides that the victim is entitled to 30 days notice of any parole eligibility hearing, and to appear and express his or her views. The victim may bring a support person to the hearing. In addition to appearing in person, the victim has the right to submit a written statement, an audiotape or videotape. The victim has the right to notice if the offender is paroled.

The victim has the right to be notified if the offender escapes.

The victim is entitled to 60 days notice if the offender is going to be placed on furlough.

COLORADO

The victim is entitled to know where the offender is incarcerated and the offender's projected release date.

The victim has the right to notification of the offender's release on furlough, work release or to a community corrections facility. The victim is entitled to notice if the offender is transferred to a non-secure facility.

The victim is entitled to notification if the offender applies for a sentence modification or post-conviction review of his or her sentence. The victim has the right to be heard at any such hearing. The victim has the right to notice of any commutation or pardon.

The victim is entitled to notice of any hearing in the appellate courts and any appellate decision.

The victim is entitled to 30 day notice of parole hearings, and to attend the hearings.

The victim is entitled to notice of the offender's release, or escape and subsequent recapture.

The victim is entitled to notice of hearings regarding revocation of the offender's probation or parole.

The victim is entitled to notice of the offender's release from a state hospital.

The victim is entitled to notice of the offender's death.

CONNECTICUT

Connecticut law provides that the victim is entitled to notice of the offender's application for sentence modification or post-conviction review and notice of hearing on the application, if one is scheduled.

The victim is entitled to notice of any parole hearings, and to participate in parole hearings.

The victim is entitled to notice of the offender's release. The victim is entitled to notice of any application for executive clemency and has the right to comment regarding such an application.

DELAWARE

Delaware law provides that the victim is entitled to notice if the offender's conviction is reversed on appeal.

The victim is entitled to notice of the offender's projected prison release date.

The victim is entitled to notice of the offender's release on work release, furlough, or other community based program.

The victim is entitled to notice if the offender escapes.

The victim is entitled to notification of the offender's parole hearing date and he or she has the right to address the board, in person or in writing. The victim is entitled to notice of the board's decision, the victim has the same rights with regard to applications for pardons.

The victim is entitled to notice of any sentence reduction or modification.

FLORIDA

Florida law provides that the victim has the right to receive notice of appellate review of the offender's conviction.

The victim is entitled to notice of any application for modification of sentence, or collateral attack upon the conviction. The victim has the right to notice if the offender escapes from a correctional institution.

The victim has the right to 30 day notice if the inmate is approved for work release.

The victim has the right to six months notice of the offender's release by parole or expiration of sentence.

Upon request, the victim is entitled to a report regarding the inmate's status.

The victim has the right to be informed of, and be present at all crucial stages, this would include all post conviction proceedings.

GEORGIA

Georgia law provides that the victim is entitled to notice of the offender's release, furlough, work release, escape or death.

The victim is entitled to 10 day notice of parole hearings and may appear personally. The board must notify the victim within 72 hours of any decision to parole the offender.

HAWAII

Hawaii law provides that the victim is entitled to 10 days notice of the offender's release on parole, or unconditional release.

The victim is entitled to notice if the offender escapes from custody.

The victim has the right to notice if the offender is released on furlough.

IDAHO

Idaho law provides that the victim has the right to be notified of any parole hearings or commutation hearings and may appear in person or submit a written statement.

The victim is entitled to notification of the offender's release or escape.

The victim is entitled to notice if the offender files an appeal.

ILLINOIS

Illinois law provides that the victim is entitled to 15 days notice of any parole hearing. The victim may make a statement at the offender's parole hearing. This statement may be made in person, in writing or by videotape. The board shall also consider any statement made by the victim at the time of trial or sentencing, and shall receive and consider any victim impact statements. The victim should be notified of the board's decision within seven days.

The victim is entitled to notice of any hearing pursuant to an application for post-conviction review or appeal. The victim is entitled to notice of any hearings regarding the appeal.

The victim is entitled to notice of the offender's final discharge or release on furlough.

The victim is entitled to notice of the offender's release from the custody of the department of mental health.

The victim is entitled to notice of the offender's release and subsequent recapture.

INDIANA

Indiana law provides that the victim is entitled to 40 days notice if the offender is scheduled for a parole hearing. If the offender has been sentenced to more than ten years, the parole board must consider the victim's opinion in deciding whether to grant parole. The victim is entitled to notice if the offender is released on parole.

The victim is entitled to notice if the offender is to be discharged from imprisonment.

The victim is entitled to notice if the offender has been approved for work release or any other type of temporary release. The victim is entitled to notice within 24 hours if the offender escapes.

The victim has the right to be informed of any application, and appear at any hearing for a commutation, pardon or reprieve.

IOWA

Iowa law provides that if the offender is confined in a local jail, the victim is entitled to notice of the offender's release or escape from custody.

If the offender is in the custody of the department of corrections the victim is entitled to notice if the offender is released on work release or a furlough, and if the offender is returning to the victim's community.

The victim is entitled to notice if the offender escapes.

The victim is entitled to notice of the offender's expected release on parole or on discharge of sentence.

The victim is entitled to be informed of the department of correction's recommendation regarding the offender's application for parole. The victim of violent crime is entitled to 20 day notice of the offender's parole hearing. The victim has the right to submit a written statement or appear personally, or through an attorney, at the hearing. The victim is entitled to notice of the board's decision.

The victim is entitled to notice of the offender's application for reprieve, pardon or commutation of sentence, and the victim may submit his or her written opinion regarding the application.

KANSAS

Kansas law provides that the victim is entitled to notice before the offender's release on parole, conditional release or expiration of sentence.

The victim is entitled to one month notice of and to be present at the public comment sessions regarding the offender's release on parole. The victim is entitled to be present at any hearings regarding an application for modification of sentence.

KENTUCKY

Kentucky law provides that the victim has the right to notice of the offender's parole hearing. The victim may submit a written impact statement for the board's consideration.

The victim has the right to notice if the offender appeals his or her conviction, the status of the appeal, and the result of the appeal.

LOUISIANA

Louisiana law provides that the victim is entitled to 30 days notice of the offender's parole hearing. The victim has the right to make a written or oral statement before the board. The victim is entitled to notice if the offender is paroled.

The victim is entitled to notice if the offender is discharged.

The victim has the right to notice if the offender appeals his or her conviction or sentence, and to be notified of arguments before the appellate courts.

The victim is entitled to notice of any modification of the offender's sentence.

The victim is entitled to notification of the offender's maximum and minimum terms of imprisonment.

The victim's family is entitled to notification of the time and place of the offender's execution and a member of the family has the right to be present at the execution.

The victim is entitled to notice if the offender escapes and also when he or she is recaptured.

MAINE

Maine law provides that the victim has the right to be informed if, when, and where the offender is going to be released from custody, on furlough, or on work release.

MARYLAND

Maryland law provides that the victim has the right to notice of post-sentencing proceedings.

The victim has the right to be notified by parole authorities of parole hearings. The victim has the right to comment in writing on any application for parole, and has the right to be notified of any decision made by the board. The victim has the right to have his or her victim impact statement read at any hearing to consider temporary leave status or a provisional release.

The victim has the right to notice of the offender's scheduled release.

The victim has the right to be informed if the offender escapes.

The victim is entitled to notice of any post-conviction review of the offender's sentence and any motion to modify or vacate the sentence.

The victim is entitled to notice of any application for commutation or remission of a sentence, or any application for pardon. He or she may submit an updated victim impact statement for consideration and may also meet with a commission member, if such an application is filed.

MASSACHUSETTS

Massachusetts law provides that the victim is entitled to 30 days notice of the offender's parole hearing. The victim may appear in person at the hearing, or submit a written statement regarding the offender's parole. The victim may also have information regarding the impact of the crime that is submitted at sentencing included in the parole board's records.

The victim is entitled to notice if the offender is released from custody.

The victim is entitled to notice if the offender escapes.

MICHIGAN

Michigan law provides that the victim has the right to notification of the offender's earliest release date or earliest parole eligibility date. The victim has the right to address the parole board, or submit a written statement, and the right to notice of the decision of the parole board. The victim may be represented by counsel at the parole hearing.

The victim has the right to notice of the offender's transfer to a minimum security facility, release to a community residential program or furlough.

The victim has the right to notification if the offender's minimum sentence is reduced due to overcrowding.

Victims of violent crimes have the right to notice of the offender's escape.

The victim has the right to 90 days prior notice of the offender's release.

The victim has the right to notice of the public hearing regarding the offender's application for reprieve, pardon or commutation of sentence, and notice if it is granted.

The victim has the right to notice if the offender appeals his or her conviction, an explanation of the appeals process, whether the defendant will be released on bail during the appeal, the time and place of any appellate proceedings and the results of the appeal.

MINNESOTA

Minnesota law provides that victims have the right to notification if the offender seeks a pardon. If such an application is made, the victim has the right to make an oral statement or submit a written statement regarding the harm caused by the crime.

65

The victim has the right to prior notification of the offender's release on furlough or placement in a work release program.

The victim has the right to prior notification if the offender is to be released from a mental hospital or other facility, or if the offender is to be placed in a facility with lower security. The victim of a crime against the person has the right to know the conditions of the release, and who will be supervising the release.

The victim has the right to notice of the offender's escape and recapture.

MISSISSIPPI

The victim is entitled to notice if the offender makes application for parole. If parole is granted, the victim is entitled to notice of the offender's release.

MISSOURI

Missouri law provides that the victim is entitled to notice of the offender's temporary, provisional or final release from custody.

The victim has the right to notice of any parole hearing scheduled for the offender, and has the right to appear personally at such hearing or to submit a written statement. The victim may have a support person attend the hearing as well. At the victim's option, the offender may be excluded during the victim's testimony. The victim may have a personal meeting with a parole board member.

The victim has the right to notice of the offender's release or escape from custody.

MONTANA

Montana law provides that the victim is entitled to notice of the term of imprisonment imposed on the offender, and the offender's release from imprisonment.

Any witness, including the victim, may appear and address the parole board regarding the offender's parole.

Notice of hearings on applications for executive clemency must be published.

NEBRASKA

Nebraska law provides that the victim is entitled to notice of any subsequent judicial proceedings if the defendant is found not guilty by reason of insanity.

The victim is entitled to notice of the tentative release date and earliest parole date of the offender.

The victim is entitled to notice of the offender's parole hearing, and the victim has the right to testify before the board or submit a written statement, and to be notified of the board's decision. The victim also has the right to notification if the offender who is paroled is returned to custody.

The victim of a sex offender has the right to notice when the offender is released from custody or from treatment.

The victim is entitled to notice if the offender is granted a furlough or release from incarceration for 24 hours or longer or when the offender is released to any community based program.

The victim is entitled to notice when the offender escapes and is recaptured.

The victim is entitled to notice when the offender is discharged from custody at the termination of his or her sentence.

NEVADA

Nevada law provides that the victim is entitled to notice when the offender is released from prison.

The victim is entitled to notice if the offender escapes.

The victim is entitled to 15 days notice of parole hearings, and may submit a written statement or appear in person.

The victim is entitled to notice if the offender receives executive clemency.

NEW HAMPSHIRE

New Hampshire law provides that the victim is entitled to notice if the offender appeals, an explanation of the appeals process, the time and place of the appeals hearing, and the result of the appeal.

The victim has the right to receive notice of and to attend sentence review hearings.

The victim has the right to receive notice if the offender escapes, is transferred or released.

The victim has the right to 15 day notice of parole hearings. The victim may submit a written statement for consideration by the board, or may appear personally or through counsel and express his or her views at the hearing. The victim has the right to be notified of the board's decision.

NEW JERSEY

New Jersey law provides that the victim has the right to include a statement in the parole report to be considered by the Board. The victim may appear in person and testify as well.

NEW MEXICO

New Mexico law provides that the victim has the right to notice if the offender receives a temporary, provisional or final release from incarceration.

The victim is entitled to notice if the offender escapes.

The victim has the right to notification of the time and place of any probation or parole hearing.

NEW YORK

New York law provides that the victim is entitled to notice of the maximum and minimum terms of the offender's imprisonment.

The victim is entitled to notice of a reversal or modification of the judgment by an appellate court.

The victim is entitled to notice of the offender's discharge, parole, and escape from prison, as well as his recapture.

When considering parole, the parole board must consider any written statement submitted by the victim.

NORTH CAROLINA

North Carolina law provides that the victim of a Class G or more serious felony is entitled to notice before any proceeding is held at which the release of the offender is to be considered.

The victim of a Class G or more serious felony is entitled to notice if the offender escapes from custody.

NORTH DAKOTA

North Dakota law provides that the victim is entitled to notice when the offender receives a provisional, temporary or final release from custody.

The victim is entitled to notice if the offender escapes.

The victim is entitled to notice if the offender is transferred to a work release program, a community residential program or to a mental health facility.

The victim may submit a written statement for consideration by the parole board. The victim of violent crime may, at the discretion of the parole or pardon board, appear personally and make a statement regarding the offender's application for pardon or parole. The victim has the right to receive notice of the parole board's decision, and the date of the offender's release, prior to any such release.

OHIO

Ohio law provides that the victim is entitled to three weeks notice if the offender is being considered for a pardon, commutation of sentence or parole. The victim has the right to comment in writing regarding the crime and the application. The victim has the right to notice if the offender is granted a parole, pardon or a commutation of sentence. If a victim impact statement was given at sentencing, that statement shall be sent to the parole authority.

The victim is entitled to notice of any action that will result in the offender being released from imprisonment prior to the expiration of his or her sentence.

The victim is entitled to notice if the offender is granted a furlough.

The victim of a violent offense is entitled to notice if the offender escapes.

OKLAHOMA

Oklahoma law provides that victims are entitled to 20 days notice of the offender's parole hearing and must be granted at least five minutes for oral testimony at the hearing. The victim is entitled to written notice of the parole board's decision within 20 days of the hearing. The board must also consider any victim impact statement given at the time of sentencing. If the victim did not receive proper notice, he or she may apply to have the decision voided.

The victim is entitled to notice when the offender completes his or her sentence, and of the offender's discharge from custody.

The victim is entitled to notice if the offender is placed on electric monitoring, house arrest or a specialized supervision program.

The victim is entitled to notice if the offender's sentence is overturned, remanded for a new trial or modified.

OREGON

Oregon law provides that the victim is entitled to 30 days notice of the offender's parole hearings and has the right to appear personally or by counsel or to submit a written statement regarding the crime and the offender.

The victim is entitled to notice of hearings and of the conditional discharge, release or escape of an offender who was found "guilty except for insanity."

The victim is entitled to 30 days notice of any release of the offender from custody.

PENNSYLVANIA

Pennsylvania law provides the victim has the right to present a statement to the parole board to be considered at the offender's parole hearing, or to appear personally before the board and testify. The victim is entitled to 10 days prior notice of the hearing, and notice of the final decision.

The victim may provide prior comment regarding the offender's possible release on furlough or work release.

The victim is entitled to notice if the offender escapes.

The victim is entitled to notice if the offender is committed to a mental health facility, and if the offender is transferred, released, or escapes from that facility.

RHODE ISLAND

Rhode Island law provides that the victim has the right to appear at the offender's parole hearing and may address the board regarding the offender's possible parole. The victim is entitled to prior notice of the offender's release on parole or any other release from custody.

SOUTH CAROLINA

South Carolina law provides that the victim is entitled to 30 days notice of the offender's parole hearing.

The victim is entitled to notice when the offender receives a temporary, provisional or final release from custody.

The victim is entitled to notice if the offender escapes.

SOUTH DAKOTA

South Dakota law provides that the victim is entitled to notice of any hearing at which a reduction of sentence will be considered. The victim may appear personally and comment regarding the impact of the crime at such a hearing.

The victim is entitled to 10 days notice of the offender's parole hearing and may be present at the hearing and may state his or her opinion regarding the offender's possible parole. The victim is entitled to notice if the inmate is granted parole.

The victim is entitled to notice if the offender escapes.

The victim is entitled to notice of the offender's release, furlough, or participation in a work release program.

TENNESSEE

Tennessee law provides that the victim is entitled to 14 days notice of the offender's parole hearing, and notice of the board's decision within 30 days. If the victim does not receive proper notice he or she may request that the board postpone the hearing, to give the victim a chance to attend and submit a statement. If the hearing has already been held, the board may consider the statement and reconsider the parole decision in light of the statement.

The victim is entitled to notice of any decision permitting the offender's release, including executive clemency.

TEXAS

Texas law provides that the Texas Department of Criminal Justice secure information relative to the offender, including written comments of his or her victims, for review by the parole board. The victim is entitled to notice if the offender is being considered for parole and is entitled to submit a written statement. The victim is entitled to notice of the offender's release on parole.

UTAH

Utah law provides that the victim may attend parole hearings and parole revocation hearings if the offender is also present. The victim may choose to observe or make an oral statement, or present a written statement. The victim may have a support person present and may testify outside the presence of the offender. The victim is entitled to notice of the offender's release on parole.

The victim is entitled to notice if the offender is released from custody, released to a halfway house, released to a rehabilitation program, or released to a state hospital.

The victim is entitled to notice if the offender is transferred to an out of state facility.

The victim is entitled to notice of the offender's escape.

VERMONT

The parole board may, in its discretion, hear testimony from interested parties. It may require them to submit statements in writing. The victim is entitled to notice of the offender's parole or release, or if the offender escapes.

VIRGINIA

Virginia law provides that the victim has the right to submit a written statement to the Virginia parole board regarding the impact of the crime, and the victim's opinions regarding the possible release of the offender.

The victim is entitled to notice of the release or discharge of the offender.

WASHINGTON

Washington law provides that the victim is entitled to notice when an offender acquitted due to insanity is granted a conditional release, a final discharge, a furlough or a transfer to a facility that is less restrictive than the state hospital. The victim is also entitled to notice if the offender escapes.

The victim is entitled to 10 day notice of the parole, release, community placement, furlough or work release of any other offender.

The victim is entitled to notice if the offender escapes.

WEST VIRGINIA

West Virginia law provides that the victim is entitled to notice if the offender escapes.

The victim is entitled to notice of the offender's release to work release, home confinement, parole or furlough.

The victim has the right to 30 days notice of the offender's release date or parole hearing.

WISCONSIN

Wisconsin law provides that the victim is entitled to notice of the conditional release, termination or discharge of an offender found not guilty by reason of mental disease or defect.

The victim is entitled to notice if the offender applies for a pardon. He or she may submit a written statement to be attached to the application.

The victim has the right to notice of the offender's application for parole. The victim may submit a written statement regarding the application.

WYOMING

Wyoming law provides that the victim has the right to make a statement at any hearing for a correction or reduction of sentence. The victim is entitled to notice of the release of the offender, the offender's assignment to work release, and any modification of the offender's parole.

The victim is entitled to notice if the offender escapes, and of his recapture and of his death.

The victim is entitled to notice of all post-conviction hearings.

CHAPTER 5

VICTIM COMPENSATION FUNDS

Victoria had to work late on an important project. It was eleven P.M. and her building was deserted when she was finally ready to leave. On the way to her car, in the company parking garage, she was brutally attacked by two knife-wielding men. She cooperated with them when they demanded her purse, but nevertheless they stabbed her repeatedly and left her for dead, making their getaway in Victoria's new car. Victoria, barely alive, was found the next morning by the garage attendant, who immediately summoned medical assistance and the police.

Victoria's assailants used her keys to enter her house, which they located by looking at the address on her driver's license. They stole her jewelry and some electronic equipment and then vandalized the home. It was this senseless destruction that led to their capture, as they left fingerprints throughout the house. When she recovered from her wounds, Victoria learned that one of her attackers was a 35 year old parolee, and the other was the 22 year old son of a wealthy banker. Both men were tried and convicted. The older man was sentenced to 30 years in prison, the younger to 15.

Victoria was hospitalized for three weeks. Her attack left her emotionally traumatized and without the use of her right arm. She attended the sentencing hearing and told the judge about the harm the two men had caused, both financial and emotional. The judge ordered that the defendants pay Victoria's medical bills, lost wages, the cost of psychological counseling and for Victoria's vocational rehabilitation. Victoria was told that they would earn 30 cents a day working in the prison industries.

Is Victoria's only hope for compensation that her attackers will be paroled and get jobs?

No. Restitution is a prominent feature of most state sentencing codes, and courts seek to rehabilitate criminals and help their victims through restitution programs. However, restitution is often not practical, and victims waiting for criminals to compensate them often face a long wait indeed. The costs associated with violent crime frequently go far beyond what anyone reasonably expects that a criminal will ever pay.

To assist victims like Victoria, states have established victim compensation funds. It is considered a matter of good public policy to try to provide financial assistance for the victims of violent crime, just as a state might provide assistance to the victims of a natural disaster. A crime victim may file for compensation in the state where he or she was harmed, or in the state of his or her residence, if the other state does not provide compensation.

Victim compensation funds are funded in a variety of ways, such as by fees and fines assessed and collected by the criminal courts, charitable donations, proceeds collected pursuant to Son of Sam laws, and tax dollars.

Who is eligible to receive payment from a victim compensation fund?

The actual victims of violent crime are the primary beneficiaries of crime victim compensation funds. Most states define victims of violent crime as those who are injured or killed as the result of criminal action. They most often require that the victim have suffered actual physical harm as a result of the crime. However, some states have a broad definition of actual physical harm, including those who suffer nervous shock or extreme mental distress as a result of the crime. This does not mean a person who is merely upset, but one who is in such distress such that he or she suffers a substantial disorder of emotional processes, thought processes, or cognition, to the extent that it impairs his or her judgment, behavior or ability to cope.

Spouses, minor children and in some cases, adult relatives of crime victims who are killed, or who are rendered unable to work by the crime are eligible to apply for compensation. Laws establishing the funds provide that persons who are economically dependent on the victim may make claims for their loss of support. Additionally, if the victim did not earn income, but provided services for the dependents, those dependents may make a claim for loss of services. For example, the husband of a homemaker killed or disabled by a violent crime might make a claim for the cost of child care.

Many state victim compensation funds extend their assistance to persons who are injured trying to prevent a crime, trying to assist a crime victim, or who are hurt or killed while attempting to apprehend or subdue a criminal offender or while assisting the police in any other way.

Victim compensation funds may also pay persons who have provided services to the crime victim, or who have helped with the victim's crime-related expenses, such as friends who have voluntarily paid the victim's medical or funeral bills. This does not, however, apply to insurance companies or others who have a contractual or other legal obligation to provide services or indemnify the victim.

What sort of expenses will the fund pay?

When making an award, the crime victims compensation board will consider the actual and reasonable costs of the crime to the victim. Unfortunately, the board will probably be unable to fully compensate the crime victim, as every state limits the entire award that may be made, and many states place limits on the various award categories. For example, most states limit the award for funeral expenses to no more than $2,000.

Victim compensation funds may pay the reasonable and necessary costs of the victim's medical care. This includes hospital bills, drugs and medications, doctor bills, ambulance bills, the costs of eyeglasses, dentures, hearing aids and prosthetic devices. It also includes the cost of physical therapy, occupational therapy, and chiropractic care, and may also include home health care services. If the victim of a crime is disabled, the fund may compensate him or her for job retraining or for the costs associated with adapting to his or her old job with new disabilities.

The cost of burial or cremation may be covered by the fund.

The crime victim or his or her dependents may make a claim for the loss of income that resulted from the crime.

If the crime victim provided valuable services to his or her family, such as housekeeping or child care, his or her dependents may make a claim for the cost of replacing those services.

Crime victims often require psychological or psychiatric services to assist in their recovery from violent crime, and the funds recognize that these needs are as valid as the cost of medical care. Additionally, some states provide funds for the counseling expenses of the immediate family of homicide victims.

What about Victoria's pain and suffering. Can she recover compensation for that?

Probably not. Most funds do not provide compensation for losses that do not have a dollar value, such as pain and suffering, or emotional trauma. However a few states, such as Connecticut and California, provide that crime victims should be compensated for mental anguish and pain and suffering.

Will the state pay to have Victoria's home repaired?

It is possible, but not likely. Most states earmark their victim compensation funds to address the results of physical violence, and do not provide compensation for the victims of property crimes. However, Kansas and Colorado are exceptions to this rule, as they also provide compensation to the victims of property crimes.

Some states will cover property loss if it associated with a crime of violence. For example, the state of Iowa has some interesting provisions for compensating property loss when it is associated with violent crime. It allows up to $1,000 for cleaning a residence if it is the scene of a homicide, and $100 for clothing that is retained by the police as evidence.

What must Victoria do to file a claim?

Each state has its own method for processing compensation claims. Victoria should gather all her bills and medical records to document her medical expenses. She should also itemize her lost wages and any other expenses or losses incurred in connection with the crime. She will need to give the claim board information to establish that a crime did occur, such as copies of the police reports, or at least a case number. Many states have claim forms that will set out the necessary documentation. They will not process the claim if necessary documents are missing.

Some claims for compensation can be handled in a summary manner, and may only require that a claim form be filed with supporting documentation. However, if the claim is challenged, Victoria will have the opportunity to appear at a hearing. At such a hearing, evidence is taken to determine if the claim should be allowed or not. Victoria should be prepared to present any witnesses or documentary evidence that is relevant to the claim. Most committees or hearing officers will issue subpoenas on behalf of claimants who need to compel the attendance of witnesses. In addition, the witnesses may be required to bring documents in their possession that are important to the victim's claim.

In some states, if the claimant goes through the claim procedure and is not satisfied with the results, he or she may ask the state court system to review the findings of the compensation board. However, not all states provide for this kind of review.

Victoria was asked to sign a medical release form, to allow the compensation committee to review her medical records. Should she do it?

Yes. Under normal circumstances, information contained in medical records is completely confidential, and a physician who divulges this information without the patient's permission is guilty of unethical conduct and could be disciplined. However, when a claim for compensation is filed, the reviewing committee may be allowed access to those records if the claimant's medical condition is relevant to the claim. Additionally, many compensation boards have the authority to require that the victim submit to further medical tests to verify his or her claim, or even order the autopsy of a deceased victim, if necessary.

If there is information of a sensitive nature in Victoria's records that has no bearing on her claim, she might seek a determination that the commission will only receive information relevant to the claim and that her doctor will not release her entire file. For example, information about a mental disorder she suffered years ago would have no relevance to her claim for vocational rehabilitation because of the loss of the use of her arm.

Victoria's medical insurance covered all of her hospital bills. Can Victoria still make a claim for those bills against the fund?

No. Sometimes there are other sources of compensation for crime related losses, most often in the form of insurance. Crime victim compensation funds are meant to be the last, not the first, resource of victims. Any insurance payments or restitution that the victim receives reduces the amount that may be claimed from the fund. This is generally referred to as payment from "collateral sources." Other types of payment that are deemed to have come from "collateral sources" are payments from government agencies, worker's compensation payments, disability insurance payments, life insurance payments, Medicare and Medicaid payments, and payments made through Social Security disability programs. Money received from the offender in the form of restitution, or payments on a civil judgment, are also considered to be from a "collateral source."

Victoria sued her attackers and received a substantial judgment. Although she hasn't yet collected anything, it is possible that the younger offender's father is going to make a large payment on the award, in hopes that it will help his son's chances for parole. What if Victoria recovers her losses from the fund and then receives this payment?

She will be required to reimburse the fund from the payment on her judgment. Many laws give the fund "subrogation" rights. This means that once the victim receives compensation from the fund, the fund has the legal right to "stand in the victim's shoes" and enforce his or her legal rights, and collect payments made, at least up to the amount paid by the fund. In some cases, these subrogation rights also mean that the fund may bring legal action against the offender or anyone else legally liable to the victim for compensation.

The states of Alaska, Hawaii, Illinois, and Nebraska specifically exempt the proceeds from life insurance policies from their subrogation rights. This means that in the event the victim of a crime dies, and his or her survivors receive money from a life insurance policy, the state fund will not be able to seek reimbursement from those proceeds.

The states of Connecticut, Delaware, the District of Columbia, Iowa, New Jersey, New Mexico, Rhode Island, Tennessee, Vermont, Washington, Wisconsin and Wyoming limit their subrogation rights to money due the victim from the offender, such as funds from restitution orders, Son of Sam laws and civil judgments.

Are there any crime victims who are not eligible for compensation?

Yes. Laws providing for compensation to crime victims exclude certain categories of crime victims, on the grounds that it would be contrary to good public policy for some victims to be awarded state funds.

At one time, many funds denied compensation to crime victims if their attacker was a member of their household. These victims were excluded on the theory that an award to the victim would benefit the offender. However, many of those laws have been changed because it made the victims of crimes such as child abuse or domestic violence ineligible.

For the most part, these laws now prohibit awards in circumstances under which the award would benefit the offender or an accomplice of the offender, instead of making a blanket exception to family or household members.

A person who is injured while helping perpetrate a violent crime is not eligible to collect compensation from the state for his or her injuries. And many state laws also deny compensation to crime victims if they have ever committed a serious crime, on the grounds that other crime victims are more deserving of limited state resources. Some funds deny compensation to persons who are the victims of violent crime while incarcerated or while they are on parole or probation.

If the crime victim compensation board finds that the victim was responsible, entirely or partially for his or her injuries, the board may deny compensation, or reduce it in proportion to the responsibility borne by the victim. For example, the victim of an assault might not be awarded compensation for his or her medical bills if the board finds that the victim provoked the assault by insulting language or threatening gestures.

If the victim refuses, without good cause, to assist in the apprehension or the prosecution of the perpetrator of the crime, he or she will usually be ineligible to collect from the victim compensation fund.

Some state compensation funds do not award compensation to crime victims who are not placed in actual financial need by the crime, even though those victims incur expenses. For example, in Indiana, persons with a net worth of more than $200,000 are not eligible for compensation from the state.

Some states will not consider small claims. For example, the Louisiana law provides that claims for less than $250 must be rejected, while in Indiana, Oregon, Pennsylvania, South Carolina, Tennessee and Virginia, a claim will not be considered unless the victim had at least $100 of loss.

What if Victoria's attackers had never been caught, or if they were acquitted? Would Victoria have been denied compensation from the fund?

No. A victim is eligible for compensation even if the perpetrator of the crime is never caught or convicted. This is especially true in a case like Victoria's, where there is no question that she was a crime victim.

Some crime victims, such as rape victims, don't report the crime to the police. Does this affect a claim for compensation?

Yes. Almost every state requires that the crime be promptly reported to law enforcement authorities. Furthermore, the crime must have been reported within the time limits set by state law. For example, a state might require that the crime be reported within 72 hours of its occurrence.

Some states make special provision for children who are the victims of sexual offenses, since these crimes often go unreported until long after they occurred. For example, Montana law provides that a claim may be made by or on behalf of a minor victim of a sexual offense within one year of the report of the crime, or within one year of the child's eighteenth birthday, whichever is later.

The compensation committee found that Victoria was entitled to payment, but they didn't award her enough to cover all her bills. Doesn't she have the right to be compensated in full?

No.Unfortunately, there is never enough money to go around to all those harmed by crime. For that reason, every state sets limits on the amount of compensation that can be awarded, and there is no requirement that the commission make awards if it does not have the funds to do so. Some state laws provide that the claims of crime victims are settled in chronological order, as funds become available.

Victoria found it necessary to hire a lawyer to file her claim and present her case. Does she have to bear her legal expenses personally?

That depends on the law in her state. Some states provide that the fund will provide attorney fees in addition to the damages awarded, in proportion to the amount awarded.

The following states provide for the award of attorneys fees: Alaska, California, Delaware, District of Columbia, Idaho, Kansas, Louisiana, Montana, Nebraska, Nevada, New Jersey, New York, North Dakota, Ohio, Rhode Island, South Carolina, Tennessee, Texas and West Virginia.

In the states of Connecticut, Hawaii, Indiana, Massachusetts, Missouri, Utah and Wisconsin there is a statute allowing attorneys' fees. But in these states the fees are taken out of the award, and are not in addition to the award.

Are there time limits for filing a claim against the fund?

Yes. If you are the victim of a crime, you should file your claim as soon as possible. If you miss the deadline for filing a claim, and don't have a valid reason for missing it, you will not be able to pursue compensation from the fund.

Victim Compensations Funds, State by State

A Note on Award Limits:

Each state handles award limits in its own way. Some set limits on certain categories of losses, but not every state limits the same categories. If a type of loss is not mentioned in the award limit section, this does not mean that the state does not make awards of that type. It simply means that there is not a specific limit for that type of loss. In these states, the total award limit contained in the statute controls.

ALABAMA

The Law: Code of Alabama Sections 15-23-1 through 15-23-23.

Where to File: The Alabama Crime Victims Compensation Commission.

Time Limits: Police report within 72 hours of the crime. Claim within one year of the injury or death of the victim, unless the commission finds that there was good reason for the failure to report or file within the time limit.

Award limits: Lost wages or services, $200 per week; Funeral expenses, $3,000; Total,$10,000.

ALASKA

The Law: Alaska Statutes Sections 18.67.010 through 18.67.180.

Where to File: The Alaska Violent Crimes Compensation Board.

Time Limits: Police report within five days of the crime or within five days of when the report reasonably could have been made. Claim within two years of the injury or the death.

Award limits: $25,000 per victim, per incident; $40,000 total compensation to dependents, in the case of the victim's death.

ARKANSAS

The Law: Arkansas Code Sections 16-90-701 through 16-90-718.

Where to File: The Arkansas Crime Victims Reparation Board.

Time Limits: Police report, within 72 hours of the crime. Claim within a year of the injury or death.

Award limits: $1,000 future economic loss, $10,000 total.

CALIFORNIA

The Law: California Government Code Sections 13959 through 13969.2.

Where to File: The California State Board of Control.

Time Limits: Not specified. Claim within one year of the date of the crime.

Award Limits: Medical and mental health expenses connected with emotional injury, $10,000; Total, from $23,000 to $46,000, depending on the availability of federal funds.

COLORADO

The Law: Colorado Revised Statutes Sections 24-4.1-100.1 through 24-4.1-124.

Where to File: The Crime Victims Compensation Board in the Colorado judicial district where the crime was committed.

Time Limits: Police report within 72 hours. Claim within one year.

Award limits: Property damage, $250; Aggregate award, $10,000.

CONNECTICUT

The Law: Connecticut General Statutes Annotated Sections 54-201 through 54-218.

Where to File: The Connecticut Commission on Victim's Services.

Time Limits: Police report within five days. Claim within two years of the injury or death. These requirements may be waived for good cause.

Award limits: $15,000 for victims of personal injury; $25,000 for dependents of homicide victims. There is a $100 deductible.

DELAWARE

The Law: Delaware Code Annotated Title 11 Section 9001-9018.

Where to File: The Delaware Violent Crimes Compensation Board.

Time Limits: Police report within 72 hours. Claim within a year of the crime. The Board may waive the limits for good cause.

Award Limits: $25,000.

DISTRICT OF COLUMBIA

The Law: District of Columbia Code Sections 3-401 through 3-415.

Where to File: Office of The Mayor of the District of Columbia.

Time Limits: Police report within seven days of the crime. Claim within 180 days of the crime. These limits may be waived upon a showing of good cause.

Award Limits: Funeral expenses $2,000; Total, $25,000.

FLORIDA

The Law: Florida Statutes Sections 960.01 through 960.17.

Where to File: The Tallahassee office of the Florida Department of Legal Affairs.

Time Limits: Police report within 72 hours of the crime. Claim within one year of the crime or the death of the victim. The reporting period may be waived for good cause and the claim period may be extended up to two years after the crime.

Award Limits: $10,000 total.

GEORGIA

The Law: Code of Georgia Section 28-5-100 through 28-5-108 and Section 17-15-1 through 17-15-3.

Where to File: Persons injured or the dependents of persons killed while assisting the police or preventing crime should make their claim with the Georgia Claims Advisory Board. The victims of violent crime or their dependents should make their claim with the Georgia Crime Victim's Compensation Board.

Time Limits: Police report-persons injured while assisting the police or preventing crime should make a report of the crime within five days of the crime. Crime victims should make a report of the crime within 72 hours of the crime. Claims for persons injured while assisting the police or preventing crime should make their claim within 18 months of the injury or death. Crime victims should make their claim within 180 days of the crime or the death. This period may be extended up to two years.

Award Limits: Persons killed or injured while preventing crime or assisting the police, $5,000;Victims of violent crime $1,000.

HAWAII

The Law: Hawaii Revised Statutes Sections 351-1 through 351-70.

Where to File: Hawaii Criminal Injuries Compensation Commission.

Time Limits: Police report must be made "without undue delay." Claim within 18 months of the injury.

Award Limits $10,000 total.

IDAHO

The Law: Idaho Code Sections 72-1001 through 72-1025.

Where to File: The Idaho Industrial Commission.

Time Limits: Police report within 72 hours of the crime. Claim within one year of the crime.

Award Limits: Funeral $2,500; Lost wages $175 per week; Total $25,000.

IOWA

The Law: Iowa Code Section 912.1 through 912.14.

Where to File: Iowa Department of Justice.

Time Limits: Police report within 72 hours of the crime (this requirement may be waived). Claim within two years of the crime, the discovery of the crime, or the death of the victim.

Award Limits: Medical expenses, $10,500; Mental health care $1,500; Loss of income $2,000; Clothing held for evidence $100; Funeral $2,500; Loss of support $2,000 per person, $6,000 total. Death related counseling for spouse and children, $500 per person, $2,000 total; Residential cleaning, if scene of homicide $1,000.

ILLINOIS

The Law: 740 Illinois Compiled Statutes Sections 45/1 through 45/20.

Where to File: The Illinois Court of Claims.

Time Limits: Police report within 72 hours of the crime. Claim within one year of the crime. The court may extend the time for reporting or filing for good cause.

Award Limits: Replacement services and future earnings $1,000 per month; Funeral $3,000; Total $25,000.

INDIANA

The Law: Indiana Statutes Title 5 Sections 2-6.1-1 through 2-6.1-48.

Where to File: The Victims Services Division of the Indiana Criminal Justice Institute.

Time Limits: Police report within 48 hours of the crime. Claim within 180 days of the crime. The reporting requirement may be waived for good cause and the claim period may be extended for up to two years after the crime.

Award Limits Emergency shelter 30 days; Mental health counseling for family members of the victim $1,000; Total $10,000.

KANSAS

The Law: Kansas Statutes Section 74-7301 through 7321.

Where to File: The Kansas Crime Victims Compensation Board.

Time Limits: Police report within 72 hours (this requirement may be waived upon a showing of good cause). Claim within one year of the injury or death.

Award Limits: Funeral $2,000; Loss of income or services $200 per week; Total $25,000.

KENTUCKY

The Law: Kentucky Revised Statutes Sections 346.010 through 346.190.

Where to File: The Kentucky Crime Victims Compensation Board.

Time Limits: Police report within 48 hours of the crime. Claim within one year of the crime or the victim's death, these requirements may be waived.

Award Limits Loss of earnings or support $150 per week; Funeral $3,500; Total $25,000.

LOUISIANA

The Law: Louisiana Revised Statutes Sections 46:1801 through 1821.

Where to File: The Louisiana Crime Victims Reparation Board.

Time Limits: Police report within 72 hours of the crime. Claim within one year of the injury, death or loss. The Board may make exceptions to these rules upon a showing of good cause.

Award Limits: $10,000 total, unless the victim is permanently disabled, in which case the total limit is $25,000.

MAINE

The Law: Maine Revised Statutes Section 3360 through 3360-K.

Where to File: Maine Victims Compensation Board.

*Time Limits:*Police report within five days of the crime. Claim within one year of the loss, or within 60 days of the discovery of the loss, whichever occurs later. These requirements may be waived for good cause.

Award Limits: $5,000 total.

MARYLAND

The Law Code of Maryland Article 26A Sections 1 through 18.

Where to File: Maryland Criminal Injury Compensation Board.

Time Limits: Police report within 48 hours of the crime. Claim within 180 days after the crime, or the death of the victim. The reporting requirement may be waived upon a showing of good cause and the claim period may be extended up to two years.

Award Limits: Disability, $25,000; Medical, $45,000; Mental Health, $2,000; Total $45,000.

MASSACHUSETTS

The Law: Massachusetts General Laws Chapter 258A Sections 1 through 9.

Where to File: The Clerk of the District Court.

Time Limits: Police report must be made within 48 hours of the crime unless there is good cause for delay. This provision does not apply in cases of rape. Claim within one year of the crime. This may be extended to up to three years upon a showing of good cause.

Award Limits Funeral $2,000; Total $25,000.

MICHIGAN

The Law: Michigan Compiled Laws Section 18.351 through 18.368.

Where to File: The Michigan Crime Victims Compensation Board.

Time Limits: Police report within 48 hours of the crime. This limit may be extended for good cause. Claim within one year of the crime, or within one year of the report of the crime, in the case of minor victims of sexual abuse.

Award Limits: Loss of earnings or support $200 per week; Funeral $1,500; Total $15,000.

MINNESOTA

The Law: Minnesota Statutes Sections 611A.52 through 611A.67.

Where to File: The Minnesota Crime Victims Reparations Board.

Time Limits: Police report within five days of the crime, or within five days of when the crime reasonably could have been reported. Claim within one year of the injury or death or within one year of when the injury or death could have been discovered.

Award Limits: $50,000.

MISSISSIPPI

The Law Mississippi Code Sections 99-41-1 through 99-41-29.

Where to File: The Mississippi Department of Finance and Administration.

Time Limits: Police report within 72 hours of the crime, unless there is good cause for not making a prompt report. Claim within one year of the crime.

Award Limits: Mental health counseling $1,000; Funeral $1,000; Loss of income or loss of support $150 per week; Total $10,000.

MISSOURI

The Law: Missouri Statutes Sections 595.010 through 595.075.

Where to File: The Missouri Division of Worker's Compensation.

Time Limits: Police report within 48 hours of the crime. Claim within one year of the crime or the discovery of the crime. These requirements can be waived upon a showing of good cause for the delay.

Award Limits: Loss of earnings or support $200 per week; Funeral expenses $2,000; Total $10,000.

MONTANA

The Law: Montana Code Sections 53-9-101 through 53-9-133.

*Where to File:*The Division of Crime Control of the Montana Department of Justice.

Time Limits: Police report within 72 hours of the crime. Claim within one year of the crime. These limits may be extended.

Award Limits Mental health services for relatives of the victim-$500 per person, $1,500 per family; Funeral expenses $2,000; Total $25,000.

NEBRASKA

The Law: Nebraska Revised Statutes Sections 81-1801 through 81-1842.

Where to File: The Nebraska Crime Victims Reparation Committee.

Time Limits: Police report within three days of the crime. Claim within two years of the injury or death.

Award Limits: $10,000. This limit may be exceeded for employment related rehabilitation expenses.

NEVADA

The Law: Nevada Revised Statutes Sections 217.010 through 217.270.

Where to File: The Nevada State Board of Examiners.

Time Limits: Police report within five days of the crime, or within five days of when the crime should reasonably have been reported. This provision does not apply to minors who are victims of sexual abuse. Claim within one year of the personal death or injury. These requirements may be waived.

Award Limits: Loss of earnings-$200 per week; Funeral expenses-$1,000; Total-$15,000.

NEW HAMPSHIRE

The Law: New Hampshire Revised Statutes Sections 21-M:8-f through 21-M:8-j.

Where to File: The New Hampshire Victims Assistance Commission.

Time Limits: No mention of time limit for filing a police report. Claim within 60 days of the crime. The Commission may waive this requirement if good cause is shown for the delay.

Award Limits: $5,000 total.

NEW JERSEY

The Law New Jersey Statutes Sections 52:4B-1 through 52:4B-33.

Where to File: The New Jersey Violent Crimes Compensation Board.

*Time Limits:*Police report within three months of the crime. Claim within two years of the date of injury or death. These limits may be waived for good cause.

Award Limits: $25,000 total.

NEW MEXICO

The Law: New Mexico Statutes Section 31-22-1 through 31-22-24.

Where to File: The New Mexico Crime Victims Reparation Commission.

Time Limits: Police report within 30 days of the crime, this may be extended upon a showing of good cause. Claim within one year of the injury or death, this may be extended to up to two years.

Award Limits: $20,000 total.

NEW YORK

The Law: New York Executive Law Sections 620 through 635.

Where to File: The New York Crime Victims Board.

Time Limits: Police report within one week of the crime, unless the delay is justified. Sex offenses must be reported within a "reasonable time." Claim within one year of the crime or the discovery of the crime, or within one year of the crime-related death. The Board may extend this period for good cause.

Award Limits: Loss of earnings or support $20,000; Funeral $2,000; Personal property $100.

NORTH CAROLINA

The Law: General Statutes of North Carolina Sections 15B1 through 15B25.

Where to File: The North Carolina Crime Victims Compensation Commission.

Time Limits: Police report within 72 hours. Claim within one year of the crime. These requirements may be waived upon a showing of good cause for the delay.

Award Limits: Funeral expenses $2,000; Replacement services $200 per week for 26 weeks; Loss of income $200 per week for 26 weeks; Total $20,000 plus funeral expenses.

NORTH DAKOTA

The Law: North Dakota Century Code Sections 54-23.4-01 through 54-23.4-18.

Where to File: The Division of Adult Services of the North Dakota Department of Corrections and Rehabilitation.

Time Limits: Police report within 72 hours of crime unless there is good cause for failure to make a prompt report. Claim within one year of the injury or death, this may be extended if the interests of justice so require.

Award Limit: Loss of income and replacement service loss $300 per week; Total $25,000.

OHIO

The Law: Ohio Revised Code Sections 2745.51 through 2743.72.

Where to File: In the Court of Claims or the Court of Common Pleas.

Time Limits: Police report within 72 hours of the crime, unless there is good cause for failure to make a prompt report. Claim within two years of the crime, in the case of a minor victim, within two years of filing the criminal complaint.

Award Limits: Funeral $2,500; Total $50,000.

OKLAHOMA

The Law: Oklahoma Statutes Chapter 21, Section 142.1 through Section 142.18.

Where to File: Oklahoma Crime Victims Compensation Board.

Time Limits: Police report within 72 hours of the crime, although the Board may waive this requirement upon a showing of good cause. Claim within one year of the injury or death. The Board may waive this requirement for an additional year, but no claims will be considered after two years.

Award Limits: Work loss or loss of services $200 per week; Total $10,000.

OREGON

The Law: Oregon Revised Statutes Chapter 147, Section 005 through Section 375.

Where to File: Oregon Department of Justice.

Time Limits: Police report within 72 hours of the crime unless the Department of Justice finds that there is good cause for the victim's failure to make a report. Claim within six months of the date of injury to the victim, or within extensions allowed by the Department of Justice.

Award Limits: Medical, hospital and counseling expenses $10,000; Loss of earnings or support $200 per week, up to $10,000; Rehabilitation services $3,000; Funeral expenses $2,000; Total $23,000.

PENNSYLVANIA

The Law 71 Pennsylvania Statutes Section 180-7 through 180-7.17.

Where to File: Pennsylvania Crime Victim's Compensation Board.

Time Limits: Police report within 72 hours unless the delay is justified. Claim One year after the crime or the death; this may be extended for up to two years, and claims brought by or for minors may be brought up to five years later.

Award limits: Loss of earnings or support $15,000 (or $20,000 if the victim of the crime died); Total $35,000.

RHODE ISLAND

The Law: General Laws of Rhode Island Section 12-25-1 through 12-25-14.

Where to File: File a civil action against the State of Rhode Island in Superior Court.

Time Limits: Police report within 10 days unless the victim was under the age of 18, or of unsound mind. Claim within three years of the death or personal injury.

Award Limits: Total $25,000.

SOUTH CAROLINA

The Law Code of Laws of South Carolina Section 16-3-1110 through Section 16-3-1340.

Where to File: South Carolina Victim's Compensation Fund.

Time Limits: Police report within 48 hours unless there are special circumstances that justify the delay in reporting. Claim within 180 days of the crime or the death. May be extended for up to four years upon a showing of good cause.

Award Limits: Funeral expenses $2,000; Total $10,000.

SOUTH DAKOTA

The Law: South Dakota Codified Laws Section 23A-28B1 through 23A-28B-44.

Where to File: South Dakota Crime Victim's Compensation Commission.

Time Limits: Police report within five days of the crime, or within five days of when the crime could have been reported. Claim within one year of the personal injury or death, although this may be waived for good cause.

Award Limits: Loss of earnings or support $500 per month; Total $10,000.

TENNESSEE

The Law: Tennessee Code Section 29-13-101 through 29-13-118.

Where to File: Tennessee Division of Claims Administration.

Time Limits: Police report within 48 hours of the crime, although this may be extended for good cause. Claim within one year of the crime or death. In the case of a minor, within one year of the manifestation of the injury to the minor.

Award Limits: Pain and suffering (awarded only to the victims of sexual offenses) $3,000; Funeral expenses $3,000; Total $7,000.

TEXAS

The Law: Texas Statutes, Code of Criminal Procedure, Article 56.31 through 56.61.

Where to File: Office of the Texas Attorney General.

Time Limits: Police report within 72 hours of the crime; this may be extended for good cause, and the limitation does not apply if a child is the victim of the crime. Claim within one year of the crime; this may be extended for good cause. In the case of children, the claim should be brought within one year of a parent or guardian becoming aware of the crime.

Award Limits: Loss of earnings or support $200 per week; Child care costs from $50 for one child to $100 per week for two children, to $125 per week for three or more children; Total $25,000.

UTAH

The Law: Utah Code Section 63-63-1 through 63-63-31.

Where to File: The Utah Crime Victim's Reparations Board.

Time Limits: Police report within seven days of the crime. A reasonable extension is allowed if the victim was unable to report the crime. Claim within one year of the injury or death. An extension of up to four years may be granted for children who are the victims of the crime.

Award Limits: $25,000 total.

VERMONT

The Law: Vermont Statutes Section 13-5351 through 13-5359.

Where to File: Vermont Victim's Compensation Board.

Time Limits: The Vermont Victim's Compensation Law does not address when the crime must be reported, but a police report must be made at some time. Claim must be brought within the period of time permitted for commencing a criminal prosecution for the crime (in other words, before the Statute of Limitations on the crime runs out). This may be extended.

Award Limits: Total $10,000.

VIRGINIA

The Law: Code of Virginia Section 19.2-368.1 through 19.2-368.18.

Where to File: The Industrial Commission of Virginia.

Time Limits: Police report within 120 hours of the crime, may be extended for good cause. Claim within 180 days of the crime or the death, may be extended for up to two years.

Award Limits: Loss of wages $200 per week; Funeral expenses $2,000; Mental health counseling for survivors of homicide victim $1,000.

WASHINGTON

The Law: Revised Code of Washington, Title 7, Chapter 7.68.010 through Chapter 7.68.915.

Where to File: Washington Department of Labor and Industries.

Time Limits: Police report within one year of the crime, or within one year of when the crime could have been reported. Claim within one year of the report of the crime.

Award Limits: Temporary disability $15,000; Survivor benefits, Surviving spouse with no children, $7,500; Surviving spouse who has custody of all victim's children, burial expenses plus $7,500; Surviving spouse if some of victim's children live elsewhere-spouse receives $3,750 and the children not living with the surviving spouse divide $3,750; Total $30,000

WEST VIRGINIA

The Law: West Virginia Code Section 14-2A-1 through 14-2A-29.

Where to File: The Court of Claims.

Time Limits: Police report within 72 hours of the crime, unless there is good cause for failing to make a prompt report. Claim within two years of the crime.

Award Limits: Non-death cases $20,000; Death cases $30,000.

WISCONSIN

The Law: Wisconsin Statutes Section 9491 through Section 949.18.

Where to File: The Wisconsin Department of Justice.

Time Limits: Police report within five days of when a report could have been made. Claim within one year of the crime. This requirement may be waived.

Award Limits: Value of clothing and bedding held as evidence $300; Value of other property held as evidence $200; Costs of cleaning the crime scene $1,000; Funeral expenses $2,000; Total $40,000.

WYOMING

The Law: Wyoming Statutes Section 1-40-102 through 1-40-119.

Where to File: Wyoming Crime Victims Compensation Committee

Time Limits: Police report "as soon as practical under the circumstances." Claim within one year after the death or injury. Extensions may be granted for good cause.

Award Limits: Loss of earnings and support $500 per week.; Total $10,000.

CHAPTER 6

RESTITUTION AND "SON OF SAM" LAWS

Mark spent the Labor Day weekend fishing and camping with some friends. On Monday evening, he drove home looking forward to a long hot shower. He put his car in the garage, and went through to the kitchen. That's when he noticed that the back door leading into his kitchen was slightly ajar. He walked into the living room and saw that his stereo system and television were gone. He then checked his bedroom, and could not find his new video camera. He called the police, and an investigator was dispatched along with a fingerprint technician.

Mark was not optimistic about recovering his property, and submitted his insurance claim. He was really surprised a few weeks later when a police detective called him and told him that two young men from his neighborhood were suspected in the burglary. He asked Mark if either had been in his home with Mark's permission, as their fingerprints were found in his living room. Mark told the detective that they had never been in his home with his knowledge. The detective told him that they would be arrested and their homes would be searched.

The police did not find Mark's video camera or compact disk player, but Marks' stereo speakers were in the bedroom of one of the suspects. The young men pleaded guilty and Mark got his speakers back. He also collected insurance for the remaining property, minus his $500 deductible.

Mark didn't have to go to court when the burglars pleaded guilty, but the prosecutor told him that he would like him to prepare a statement regarding his losses and be prepared to appear at the sentencing. He told Mark he wanted him to present the court with his losses, so the judge could order restitution. Mark is relieved that his losses only added up to $500 and wonders what the point of restitution would be in his case.

Courts often have a dual purpose in mind when they enter restitution orders: to compensate crime victims without spending taxpayer's money, and to rehabilitate criminals. Under restitution plans, criminal defendants are ordered to pay back the victims of their crimes. Often times, this means that they are ordered to pay medical bills, for the replacement of stolen or damaged property, to make up for lost wages, to cover the costs of psychological counseling and, in the most tragic cases, to pay funeral expenses. The value of restitution to victims is clear; it is hoped that restitution will help them recover from the crime. Many courts also believe that payment of restitution will have a rehabilitative effect on the criminal, that it will teach him or her the consequences and impact of criminal behavior, and instill a sense of responsibility.

Mark learned that the burglars also faced charges in several other break-ins, but some of the charges were dropped in return for their guilty pleas. Will they be required to make restitution to their other victims as well?

Criminal defendants often plea bargain their cases, which means that some criminal charges are dropped in return for a plea of guilty to other charges. Some state laws, such as those of Alabama and Washington, make it clear that the court is not limited to convictions when ordering restitution, and the court can order restitution for the offenses to which the defendant admits as well.

Are criminal offenders required to make restitution in all cases?

Where restitution is not mandatory, the court will consider the needs and circumstances of the victim, the needs of the victim's dependents, and the financial resources and earning ability of the defendant. (However, in some states, the court is directed *not* to consider the defendant's economic circumstances when setting a restitution award. In those states, it is considered irrelevant, as the only standard for a restitution order should be the extent of the victim's loss.)

In the following states, the victim has the right to receive restitution as part of the disposition of the criminal case: Alabama, Arizona, Arkansas (it may be total restitution or partial), Colorado,

99

Iowa (mandatory in all cases with the exception of simple misdemeanors), Kansas (mandatory if the offender receives probation, a suspended sentence or community corrections), Kentucky (mandatory if the offender receives probation or conditional discharge), Minnesota, Missouri, New Hampshire, New Mexico (if the offender is placed on probation or paroled), Rhode Island, South Carolina (unless there are substantial and compelling reasons to not enter an order), Tennessee (if the offender receives probation or a suspended sentence, Washington (unless there are extraordinary circumstances), and Wyoming (unless it is clear to the court that the defendant will never have the ability to pay restitution).

In the following states, the victim has the right to request that an order of restitution be made part of the final disposition of the case: Florida, Hawaii, Maryland, Massachusetts, Minnesota, Missouri, and New York.

How will a victim know to come to court to request restitution?

Restitution is usually set at a separate hearing or during the sentencing hearing. In either event, the victim has the right to notice of the hearing, and to be present at the hearing. Many state codes provide specifically that they victim has the right to be heard. This means that the victim may not be prevented from making a statement and presenting evidence. Although restitution is usually set by the judge as part of the sentence imposed, in Arkansas, the jury sets the amount of restitution, with the prosecutor's recommendation.

What good is a court order directing a criminal to do anything? Will he or she really obey it?

Unfortunately, in some cases, an order of restitution can be virtually worthless; the inmate on death row won't be making any payments towards his victim's funeral bills, and the paroled burglar might only be earning minimum wage upon his release. However, if the convicted criminal has an income, the courts and victims have several tools to insure that payment of restitution is a priority:

•The law in some states provides that while the defendant is incarcerated, any income that he or she has can be used to pay restitution.

•When the inmate is paroled the parole board may condition this release upon continued payment of restitution.

•If the defendant is granted a suspended sentence or probation, failure to pay restitution can be a violation of the conditions of probation or the suspended sentence. In these cases, these violations may result in the defendant being incarcerated or re-incarcerated.

If the burglars are released and working, what is the best way for Mark to collect his money?

Mark may be able to work with the prosecutor or the probation or parole officer to keep tabs of restitution payments, and remind the offenders that they could be incarcerated if they don't meet their obligation. However, the collection of restitution must often take a back seat in busy district attorneys' offices to the prosecution of crime.

In most cases, crime victims don't have to rely on probation or parole officers, or the prosecutors to enforce their restitution orders. Many states grant crime victims the right to enforce their judgments on their own: Alabama, Alaska, Arizona, Arkansas, California, Colorado, Delaware, Georgia, Idaho, Illinois, Indiana, Iowa, Maryland, Michigan, Minnesota, Mississippi, Missouri, Nebraska, New Jersey, Rhode Island, South Carolina, South Dakota, Texas, Utah, Vermont, Washington, West Virginia and Wisconsin.

In these states the law provides that a restitution order should be treated as any final judgment in a civil case. This means that a victim who has been granted a restitution order may take legal steps, such as wage garnishments or executions on property, to satisfy the judgment. Some special provisions of these laws include:

•In California, a restitution order accumulates interest at the rate of 10% per annum. In Oklahoma, the interest rate is 12% per annum.

•In Colorado and Rhode Island the victim may collect attorney fees incurred in enforcing his or her lien.

- In Delaware, the court may require that the defendant execute a wage assignment to pay the victim's restitution.
- In Alabama, California, Florida, and Washington the court may enter an income withholding order.
- In Alaska, if an offender is imprisoned for failing to pay ordered restitution, he or she receives a "credit" of $50 per day towards satisfaction of the order. In Oregon, the "credit" is $25 per day.
- In Maine, if the offender is on work release, up to 25% of his or her income is allocated for restitution.
- In New Jersey, the failure to pay restitution is grounds for the court to revoke an offender's driver's license.

What about offenders who can't find jobs? Will they have to go to jail for failure to pay?

No. If the offender truly cannot find employment, the court will not find that he or she is wilfully violating the restitution order. However, a few states have tried to remedy this situation.

In Delaware, the offender may be referred to a work program. In Illinois, if the crime resulted in damage to property, and the defendant has sufficient skills, he or she may repair the property personally, in lieu of paying the cost of repairs. Mississippi operates a community service restitution program. The victim has the right to provide input and make comments as to whether or not the offender should be allowed to participate in such a program.

Must the offenders pay their restitution immediately?

In most situations, it would be a waste of time to order the criminal to pay amounts due the victim immediately. They rarely have funds or property, and it is unlikely that they could get a loan to cover the restitution. For this reason, the court usually sets a schedule for payments, taking into account the defendant's earning ability and other obligations.

The police detective told Mark that he had the right to sue the offenders for trespass, in the civil courts. Mark wondered why any victim would go to the time and trouble to sue, once he or she had a restitution order.

In the following states, law enforcement is required to inform the victim that in addition to receiving an order of restitution, the victim has the right to sue the offender in civil courts for damages: Colorado, North Carolina, and Wyoming.

As to Mark's question, in most states the court does not have the authority to order restitution to compensate a victim for his or her pain and suffering or mental anguish or punitive damages. In a civil action, the victim can get a judgment for these more intangible damages. In restitution cases, the court usually must stick to out of pocket expenses. While not really relevant in Mark's case, it may be important in a crime of violence, especially if an escrow account might be established, pursuant to the "Son of Sam" laws.

Is there any hope for the victim of an incarcerated offender?

If the offender is in jail, restitution payments probably won't be arriving very quickly. However, some states do have special provisions for payment by inmates:

- In New Hampshire, if an incarcerated offender is earning wages, through work release or other prison-related employment, the court may order that his or her wages be turned over to the Department of Corrections. That money is then used for the prisoner's maintenance, the support of his or her dependents, and restitution.
- In Hawaii, 10% of a prisoner's annual earnings may be set aside for restitution.
- The Louisiana Department of Corrections operates the Louisiana Restitution Industries for inmates. After deductions for taxes and social security, 30% of the inmate's wages goes towards victim restitution.
- The Tennessee Department of Corrections operates Residential Restitution Centers. The inmate's wages are turned over to the Department. The Department pays the inmate's boarding costs and then reimburses the victim according to the terms of a restitution contract. Tennessee also operates a restitution industries program. Under this program, from 5% to 20% of the inmate's wages go to restitution.

•Oregon work release programs provide that the inmate's earnings are earmarked for the support of his or her dependents, and restitution.

What exactly are "Son of Sam Laws"?

In 1977, after a year of murder and mayhem, the New York City police arrested a man who had held the city captive for months. His name was David Berkowitz, and he was accused of being the notorious .44 calibre killer or the "Son of Sam" who had left six people dead and another seven people wounded.

He captured the attention of the entire country during his killing spree, partially because he hunted down and shot young, pretty girls and their companions. At the time of his arrest, he was in possession of a machine gun, and was on his way to a disco, planning to open fire on the crowd. By that time, the media attention was so great that one person commented that there would be people "...waiting at the precinct house, to get him to sign a contract." In fact, Berkowitz was paid $75,000 by one publishing company for the rights to his story.

The fact that a killer could actually profit by recounting his crimes outraged New York legislators to such an extent that they passed the first "Son of Sam Law." This was their attempt to insure that in the future crime wouldn't pay. Under this law, and "Son of Sam" laws now enacted in nearly all the states, a criminal cannot profit from his or her crime by selling book or movie rights. Any money owing the criminal is instead placed in a fund for the benefit for the victims of the crime(s).

A typical "Son of Sam" law provides that anyone who contracts with a convicted felon, or with a criminal defendant to reenact his or her crime in a movie, book or other type of media, such as sound recordings, or to publish his or her thoughts, feelings or emotions regarding the crime shall pay any money owed to the offender to the court where the action is pending, or to a state reparation fund, or some other state agency. The money is then held in escrow for a certain period of time, to enable the victims of the offender to bring claims for restitution and damages.

New York, the state which enacted the original "Son of Sam" law, has recently made changes in its law, so that it operates in a slightly different way, although the results are very similar. Profits from literary or other arrangements do not automatically go to a special fund or escrow account. Instead, the Crime Victim's Board has the authority to apply for a court order to attach profits or establish a receivership or pursue other civil remedies to preserve the money for the victims of the offender's crimes.

What if a defendant charged in a highly publicized crime is found not guilty?

If the defendant is found not guilty, he or she is entitled to the money. However, most state laws provide that a verdict of "not guilty due to reason of insanity" or "not guilty due to diminished capacity" is to be treated as a finding of guilt under the statute.

How does a victim know if any money is available in an escrow account?

Most "Son of Sam" laws provide that the board or body that establishes and administers the account must publish notice at regular intervals, if there is money available.

For example, the Arkansas law provides that money deposited pursuant to the "Son of Sam" law be deposited with the circuit court where the charges were filed. It further directs the court to publish a notice, once a year for four years, in at least one newspaper of general circulation in each county of the state, that the money is available. The state of Mississippi allows crime victims to register with the state treasurer to insure that they will be notified in the event an escrow account is established.

If you may be due some money under a "Son of Sam" law, it's a good idea to find out who administers such accounts in your state, and then make periodic inquiries.

Are there time limits for making claims?

Yes. To protect your rights under "Son of Sam" laws, make sure that you make a claim as soon as possible. All the states have time limits for bringing a claim, and if you miss the limit, you will have no right to the funds collected under the law. The time limits start running when certain events occur, and the law varies from state to state. Under some laws the time begins to run when money is first placed in the account; under others, when the defendant is convicted, and under still others when the crime occurs.

What happens to the money if no claims are made?

Each state may make its own provisions for the disposal of uncollected funds. Under some laws, the money reverts to the state, under others, the defendant is entitled to the money if no claims are made. Other laws provide that the money goes to restitution funds, or to crime victims' compensation funds. Many states allow the offender to use funds in the account to defray the cost of his or her defense.

What must a victim do to establish his or her right to the money in the escrow account?

That depends on the state law. In some states, the victim must file a claim with the board or body administering the fund. In other states the victim should bring a civil lawsuit against the defendant and get a judgment, which is then satisfied with the funds in the account. In some states, an order for restitution is sufficient to establish a claim.

"Son of Sam" Laws State-by-State

ALABAMA

Eligible victims must bring an action within five years, if no action is brought within the time limit, the money in the fund reverts to the state.

ALASKA

Eligible victims must bring an action in civil court, or receive a restitution order within ten years of the crime, or within ten years of the discovery of the perpetrator of the crime.

ARIZONA

Eligible victims must apply for compensation within five years of the establishment of the account containing the escrowed funds.

If no claims are made within five years, the money reverts to the state.

ARKANSAS

Eligible victims must file suit within five years of the filing of the charges. The defendant may use money in the account, upon court order, in order to pay legal fees, if he or she cannot otherwise afford legal representation. If no claims are filed within the time limit, the money in the account goes to victim reparation or assistance programs.

CALIFORNIA

Eligible victims must bring an action within five years of the conviction, or five years of the establishment of the trust, (the attorney general is authorized to bring such an action on their behalf). However, the government has the first claim on money in the account, if the government has borne the expense of the accused's defense.

COLORADO

Eligible victims must bring suit within five years of the establishment of the fund. If the defendant is acquitted, or if no claims are brought, the defendant is entitled to the money in the fund.

CONNECTICUT

Eligible victims must bring a civil action against the offender within five years of the date of the crime. If no claims are filed, the money in the fund goes to the crime victim's compensation fund.

DELAWARE

Eligible victims must bring a civil action within five years from the time the account is established. The defendant may use up to 20 % of the funds in the account for his or her defense. If the defendant is acquitted, he or she is entitled to the money in the account.

FLORIDA

Twenty-five percent of the proceeds from literary, cinematic or other account of the crime are earmarked for the dependents of the convicted felon. If there are no dependents, that portion is deposited in the crime victims' compensation fund. Twenty-five percent of the proceeds are allocated for the victims of the crime. The remainder is applied to the costs of the prosecution and any remaining funds are forwarded to the crime victims' compensation fund.

GEORGIA

Eligible victims must bring a civil action for damages against the offender within five years of the establishment of the escrow account. If no action is brought, the funds go to the offender or the offender's legal representatives.

HAWAII

Money collected under the law goes first to pay the defendant's legal expenses, and then to reimburse the crime victims compensation fund for any payments made to the victims of the crime. After those payments, the money is used to satisfy any civil judgments for damages against the offender, in connection with the crime. When the statute of limitations for bringing civil actions has expired, and when there are no longer any civil actions pending, and after ten years have passed since the last action taken by a victim against the offender, any remaining money is turned over to the offender.

IDAHO

The offender may use funds in the account for legal expenses in connection with the criminal prosecution. Eligible victims must bring a civil action for damages against the offender within five years of the establishment of the account. If there are no claims, the offender gets the money.

ILLINOIS

Funds in the account may be used by the offender to pay legal expenses in connection with the criminal prosecution. Eligible victims must bring a civil action for damages against the offender within five years of the establishment of the account. If no claims are filed the funds go to the Violent Crime Victims' Assistance Fund.

INDIANA

The offender may use money in the escrow account for legal expenses in connection with the prosecution. Eligible victims must file a civil action for damages against the offender within two years of the crime. If no claims are filed within that period, the money in the account goes to the Crime Victim's Compensation Fund.

IOWA

The offender may use money in the escrow account for legal expenses in connection with the criminal prosecution. Eligible victims must bring a civil action for damages within five years of the establishment of the escrow account. Funds may also be used to satisfy restitution orders. If there are no such orders or civil actions, the offender gets the money in the account.

KANSAS

Eligible victims must bring a civil action for damages within six months of notification from the Crime Victim's Compensation Board that it has received funds pursuant to the "Son of Sam" law. They should receive a judgment from a court for their damages within two years of that notification. Money left over goes first to satisfy restitution orders, then to the Board of Indigent Defense Services for the costs of the offender's legal representation and to satisfy court costs, then to reimburse the Crime Victim's Compensation Board, and then to the State Treasury.

KENTUCKY

Money in the escrow account may be used to reimburse the Kentucky Crime Victim's Compensation Board for any payments that it has made to victims. Eligible victims must bring a civil action for damages within five years of the establishment of the account. If there are no claims from the Board or civil actions within that time, the offender is entitled to the money in the account.

LOUISIANA

The offender may use money in the account for legal expenses in connection with the criminal prosecution. Twenty-five percent of the funds are earmarked for the Louisiana Crime Victim's Reparation Fund, the remaining 75% is earmarked for the victims of the crime. If there are multiple victims, those that do not bring a civil action for damages within one year of the establishment of the account lose out to the claims of other victims. If there only one victim, he or she must bring a civil action for damages within two years of the establishment of the account. If there are no claims brought within three years of the establishment of the account, all the funds in the account go to the Crime Victim's Reparation Fund.

MAINE

No "Son of Sam" law in effect.

MARYLAND

The offender may use funds in the account for legal expenses in connection with the prosecution. Eligible victims must bring a civil action for damages against the offender within five years of the establishment of the account. If no claims are brought, the money is turned over to the offender.

MASSACHUSETTS

The offender may use funds in the account for legal expenses in connection with the criminal prosecution. Eligible victims must bring a civil action for damages within three years of the establishment of the account. If there are no claims, the offender gets the money.

MICHIGAN

Eligible victims must obtain a restitution order or civil judgment against the offender within five years of the establishment of the escrow account. If no claims are filed, 50% of the funds in the account are earmarked for the crime victims compensation board and the offender is entitled to the remaining 50%.

MINNESOTA

Eligible victims must bring a civil action for damages against the offender within five years of the establishment of the account. Funds in the account may be used by the offender for legal fees in connection with the criminal prosecution, and up to 10% of the funds may go to the offender's minor children. If no claims are filed, the remaining money goes to the Crime Victim's Reparations Board.

MISSISSIPPI

The offender may use funds in the account for legal expenses in connection with the criminal prosecution. Eligible victims must bring a civil action for damages against the offender within one year of the establishment of the account. If there are no claims, money in the account goes to satisfy any child support obligation that the offender may have and any remaining funds go to the offender.

MISSOURI

The offender may use funds in the account for legal expenses in connection with the criminal prosecution. Eligible victims must bring a civil action for damages within five years of the establishment of the account. If there are no actions filed, the money in the account goes to the Crime Victims Compensation Fund.

MONTANA

Funds in the account may be used by the offender for legal fees in connection with the criminal prosecution. Eligible victims and the dependents of deceased victims may collect their actual damages or $5,000, whichever is greater, from the account. Funds in the account are held for a period of time deemed reasonably necessary to complete their claims. Any funds left over are turned over to the Crime Victim's Assistance and Compensation Account.

NEBRASKA

The offender may use funds in the account for legal expenses in connection with the criminal prosecution. Eligible victims must bring a civil action for damages within five years of the establishment of the fund. If no claims are brought, the money in the fund goes to the offender.

NEVADA

Eligible victims must bring an action within five years of the time that the offender became legally entitled to the proceeds of a contract for the use of his or her story. If no claims are brought, the offender is entitled to the proceeds.

NEW HAMPSHIRE

No "Son of Sam" law in effect.

NEW JERSEY

Eligible victims must bring an action within five years of the establishment of the escrow account. Funds in the account go first to satisfy those claims, then to satisfy restitution orders, to cover the offender's legal fees and to satisfy other creditors, then all remaining funds are turned over to the Violent Crimes Compensation Board.

NEW MEXICO

The offender may use funds in the account for legal expenses incurred in connection with the criminal prosecution. Eligible victims must bring a civil action for damages against the offender within five years of the establishment of the account. If no claims are brought, the money in the account goes to the offender.

NEW YORK

Eligible victims must bring an action within three years of the offender receiving profits from his or her crime.

OHIO

Eligible victims must bring an action within three years of the establishment of the escrow account. If there are no claims, or if there are funds left over in the account, those funds are returned to the parties who contracted with the offender.

OKLAHOMA

The offender may use funds in the account for legal expenses incurred in connection with the criminal prosecution. Eligible victims must bring a civil action for damages within five years of the date that charges are filed against the defendant. If no claims are brought, the money in the account goes to the Victim's Compensation Revolving Fund.

OREGON

Eligible victims must bring a civil action for damages against the offender within five years of the establishment of the account. If no claims are brought, the money in the account goes to the offender.

PENNSYLVANIA

The offender may use funds in the account for legal expenses incurred in connection with the criminal prosecution. Eligible victims must bring a civil action for damages within five years of the establishment of the account. If no claims are brought, the money in the account goes to the offender.

RHODE ISLAND

The offender may use up to 20% of the money in the account for legal expenses incurred in connection with the criminal prosecution. The State may claim funds in the account for providing the offender with defense services, or for the investigation or prosecution of the crime. Eligible victims must bring a civil action for damages against the offender within three years of the last payment to the account. If no claims are brought half the money in the fund goes to the Crimes Indemnity Fund and the remaining half goes to the offender.

SOUTH CAROLINA

Eligible victims must bring a civil action for damages within five years of the date of the crime. If no claims are brought, the money in the account goes to the offender.

SOUTH DAKOTA

Eligible victims must bring a civil action for damages within five years of the establishment of the account. If no claims are brought, the money in the account goes to the offender.

TENNESSEE

The offender may use funds in the account for legal expenses incurred in connection with the criminal prosecution. Eligible victims must file a claim with the Tennessee Division of Claims Administration within five years of establishment of the account. If no claims are brought, the offender is entitled to the money in the account.

TEXAS

No "Son of Sam" law in effect.

UTAH

Funds in the account may be used to reimburse the State for expenses incurred providing legal representation for the offender. Eligible victims must bring a civil action for damages within six years of the establishment of the escrow account. If no claims are brought the offender in entitled to the money in the account.

VERMONT

No "Son of Sam" law in effect.

VIRGINIA

The offender may use up to 25% of the funds in the account for legal expenses incurred in connection with the criminal prosecution. Eligible victims must bring a civil action for damages against the offender within five years of the establishment of the account. If no claims are brought the money in the account goes to the Criminal Injuries Compensation Fund.

WASHINGTON

The offender may use funds in the account for legal expenses incurred in connection with the criminal prosecution. Eligible victims must bring a civil action for damages against the offender within five years of the establishment of the account. If no claims are brought, the offender is entitled to 50% of the funds in the account. The remaining funds go to county funds established for programs to encourage and facilitate testimony by victims and witnesses in criminal prosecutions.

WEST VIRGINIA

No "Son of Sam" law in effect.

WISCONSIN

The offender may use funds in the account for legal expenses incurred in connection with the criminal prosecution. Eligible victims must bring a civil action for damages within three years of the establishment of the account. If no claims are brought, the offender is entitled to the money in the account.

WYOMING

Eligible victims must brings a civil action for damages against the offender within five years of the establishment of the account. If no claims are brought, the offender is entitled to the funds in the account.

CHAPTER 7

RAPE VICTIMS, RAPE SURVIVORS

Susan's boyfriend called her at work on a Friday afternoon, and suggested that they meet later. They agreed to meet at a bar near Susan's apartment at about 10 P.M. Susan arrived on time, bought herself a drink, and went into the poolroom to wait for him. By 11 o'clock her boyfriend still had not arrived, and many of the bar patrons had noted and remarked on the well dressed young woman sitting by herself. Susan was friendly by nature and when one of the pool players struck up a conversation with her, she made no effort to rebuff him.

At 11:30, having no word from her boyfriend, Susan decided to leave. Her new acquaintance offered to walk her to her car. When they got to the parking lot, he showed her a gun and told her to get into his truck. Susan was afraid that he would shoot her, so she cooperated with him. He drove a few blocks away to a deserted parking garage and raped her.

After the attack, the rapist told Susan not to bother reporting the crime. He bragged that his buddies in the pool room would be sure to tell anyone who asked that Susan was clearly working as a prostitute, and that they had heard her agree to perform sex acts in exchange for money. He left her in the garage. She was terrified and felt violated, but had no physical injuries.

Susan returned to her car and drove herself to the hospital where she was examined and treated. The emergency room doctor who treated her called the police. Susan was able to identify her attacker. He was arrested and charged with rape. Susan has already heard, from the prosecutor, that her attacker claims that no rape occurred, and that Susan had agreed to engage in sex.

Susan was telling her best friend about the attack, and her friend impatiently interrupted her, stating, "I would have made him shoot me, I wouldn't let anyone do that to me." Susan

began to cry, because she had already begun to question herself, wondering if she should have fought back, or if she had given the rapist grounds to believe that she would willingly have sex with him. She doesn't know what to do, and she doesn't want to go to court in this state of mind.

It has long been remarked that women who are raped are often victimized twice, once by their attacker, and again by the legal system. Rape victims often feel that they are being put on trial when lawyers ask them questions about their conduct, their past and whether they really tried to resist. They are made to feel as if they themselves were responsible for the attacks made on them.

The rate of successful rape prosecutions is shamefully low when compared with the number that occur. This is because rapes are often not reported, and because juries frequently fail to convict defendants charged with rape. Blaming the victim is more prevalent in the case of rape than in any other crime.

Susan shouldn't give up. Her rapist should be punished for his acts, and should be put away so that he won't attack another woman. Susan should contact a support group for sexual assault victims, who can help her to see that the blame and responsibility for this attack lie with the rapist, not with her.

A police detective, investigating the crime, asked Susan a lot of questions about her relationship with her boyfriend, and past boyfriends. When she protested, he told her that she should expect those sort of questions at trial. He even asked to see the dress she was wearing when she was attacked, and commented that it was a provocative outfit. Can Susan really be questioned about her sexual relationships at trial? Should her taste in clothes be an issue in this case?

For many women, the thought that their past sexual behavior will be examined, discussed, and reviewed by strangers is a strong deterrent to lodging a rape complaint. For that reason, most states have enacted "rape shield laws." These laws prevent the defense, in rape trials (or trials for other types of sexual assault) from introducing evidence of the victim's past sexual conduct or reputation at the trial.

In addition to protecting victims from embarrassing and irrelevant questions, rape shield laws also prevent the defense from
distracting the attention of the jury from the real issue in the trial.
Rape shield laws reflect our belief that whether the victim has loose
morals or wears provocative clothing has no bearing on whether
non-consensual sexual contact occurred at a certain time and place.

Most rape shield laws have provisions that allow the defendant,
under some circumstances, to present evidence regarding the victim's
past sexual conduct. For example, if the defendant was involved in
the past sexual conduct, this might have a bearing on the issue of
consent. On the other hand, evidence of the victim's sexual relations with others has no real relevance to the issue of consent.

Some rape shield laws allow the introduction of evidence regarding past sexual conduct if it is being introduced to show how
the victim became pregnant, or contracted a sexually transmitted
disease, or to explain the presence of semen on the victim or her
clothing. Under a few laws, evidence of the victim's past sexual conduct is admissible if it tends to show that the victim had a motive for
making a false accusation of rape.

Under rape shield laws, if a defendant wishes to introduce evidence regarding the victim's prior sexual conduct, he must file a
motion ahead of time. The judge will hold a private hearing, without the jury present, and determine if the evidence is relevant and
should be admitted. If the court decides to allow the evidence, the
court will enter an order that sets the guidelines for what type of
questions may be asked, and what information presented.

**The same detective suggested to Susan that she could assist in
the investigation if she would agree to take a polygraph or lie
detector test. Susan was insulted and angry; does she have to agree
to such a test?**

No. Law enforcement agencies have no legal grounds to require that victims or suspects undergo polygraph examinations, and
the results of such examinations cannot be introduced into evidence
in court. The states of Connecticut, Illinois, Michigan, and Oregon have passed laws that absolutely prohibit law enforcement
agencies or courts from requiring that sexual assault victims submit

to polygraph testing as a condition of proceeding with a prosecution.

Laws in California and Illinois prohibit judges from ordering that rape victims undergo psychological testing. On the other hand, in Illinois, psychological evidence is admissible to bolster the victim's testimony. The Illinois law allows testimony from expert witnesses that the victim is suffering from post traumatic stress syndrome. This type of evidence would support the victim's claim that she underwent a traumatic event. In Nevada, the prosecution may introduce evidence in the form of expert testimony that the victim's conduct, behavior or condition is consistent with that of a sexual assault victim.

Susan wants to give evidence regarding her past sexual conduct, to prove that she's no prostitute. Will the rape shield law prevent her from doing so?

No, the law was designed to protect her, not to keep her from offering relevant evidence. However, if Susan wishes to present evidence regarding her good character or reputation, the defendant will probably be allowed to counter such evidence.

Susan really dreads testifying. She expects to see all the defendant's friends sitting in the courtroom, ready to accuse her of being a prostitute. Can she request that the courtroom be cleared during her testimony?

It is a basic principle of our legal system that criminal prosecutions take place in public, not in secret. It is likely that Susan will be required to give her testimony in full view and hearing of any spectator who decides to sit in on the proceedings. However, there are some exceptions to this rule:

- In Alabama, the courts have the authority to clear the courtroom of all but the persons necessary to the trial, if evidence of a obscene or vulgar nature is to be given.
- In New York, Mississippi and Utah, the court may exclude everyone except persons necessary to the case from the courtroom during sexual assault trials.

- In Massachusetts, the court may exclude the general public from a rape trial, if the defendant waives his or her right to a public trial.
- In Virginia the court may close the preliminary hearing to the public.
- In South Carolina and Virginia, the court may order that a rape victim give her testimony by deposition, instead of in open court. The victim's testimony is taken with only the judge, attorneys, defendant and court reporter present, then transcribed into written form and read to the jury at trial. The victim need not make a personal appearance before the jury.

Additionally, if any of the defendant's friends are going to give evidence in the case, they can be excluded from the courtroom until they testify.

One of the first things that occurred to Susan, as she was seeking medical assistance after the attack, was the possibility that she might have been exposed to the AIDS virus. The emergency room doctor told her that an immediate test would not help her, as she wouldn't test positive right away, even if she had contracted the virus. She suggested that Susan find out if her attacker has the virus. Can Susan force him to have an AIDS test?

Under normal circumstances, a person cannot be forced, against his or her will, to undergo testing for the Human Immunodeficiency Virus (HIV). Furthermore, those who undergo testing are usually assured of complete confidentiality regarding the test results. However, most states now have laws that enable the victim of a sexual assault to petition for a court order directing the perpetrator to undergo testing. In most cases, there must be some evidence that the sexual acts created a risk of exposure to the virus, such as the exchange of body fluids.

Some states allow the courts to order testing prior to the defendant's conviction, after charges have been filed. Other states do not authorize courts to force testing unless the defendant is convicted. If Susan's state has such a law, she may be able to require that her attacker undergo testing, and that the results of the test be released to her. In cases where the victim is a minor, the minor's guardian may initiate the request and receive the information.

In states without such laws, Susan should still request that the prosecutor contact the defense attorney to ask if the defendant will voluntarily undergo testing.

Many states provide counseling to sexual assault victims regarding the transmission of the AIDS virus and the availability of testing.

Will Susan be required to pay for the care she received at the hospital after the rape?

No. Most states have laws that provide that the state will pay the hospital and health care professionals for the cost of medical examinations and treatment of victims of sexual assault, provided that the assault was reported to law enforcement authorities.

Rape victims should always seek immediate medical attention. Even if the victim is not injured physically, a trip to the emergency room is in order. Doctors at the emergency room can gather evidence from the victims body, such as samples of blood, semen or other bodily fluids. The doctors can also provide treatment for exposure to sexually transmitted disease and provide medication or treatment for the prevention of pregnancy resulting from the rape.

Susan doesn't want her colleagues at work to know about the attack, especially in light of her attacker's defense strategy. Is it illegal for the media to report her name, or identify her in other ways?

Most states do not have laws on their books that make it illegal to identify the victim of a sexual assault. However, in most cases members of the news media, such as reporters, voluntarily protect the identity of the victim. The following states do have laws designed to protect the victim's privacy:

- •In Alaska and Connecticut, the name of victims of sexual assault remain confidential, even in court documents.
- •In Massachusetts, reports of rape, and sexual assault are confidential and any court records containing the victim's name must be withheld from public inspection.

- In Florida and South Carolina, it is illegal to publish, print or broadcast the name, address or other identifying information of a rape victim.
- In California, Connecticut and Nevada the victim must reveal her name in court, but may decline to testify regarding her home and business address or telephone number.
- In Michigan, the name of a rape victim may be suppressed until the defendant is arraigned on the charges, or until the case is dismissed or otherwise disposed of.
- In Texas, a sexual assault victim may choose to have a pseudonym used in place of his or her name in all public files and records concerning the offense, including police summary reports, press releases and records of judicial proceedings. The victim is not required to disclose his or her name, address or telephone number in connection with the investigation or prosecution. It is a class C misdemeanor, under this law for any public employee to disclose such a victim's identity.

Minnesota and Pennsylvania: Strong Protection for the Victims and Survivors of Rape

The state of Minnesota has legislation that could serve as a guide for the appropriate courtroom treatment of rape victims throughout the country. It provides:

- In a prosecution for sexual assault, the testimony of a victim need not be corroborated.
- In a prosecution for sexual assault, there is no need to show that the victim resisted the defendant.
- In a prosecution for sexual assault, the court *shall not* instruct the jury that:
  —it may be inferred that a victim who has previously consented to sexual intercourse with persons other than the defendant would be

121

therefore more likely to consent to sexual intercourse again.

—the victim's previous or subsequent sexual conduct in and of itself may be considered in determining the credibility of the victim.

—criminal sexual conduct is a crime easily charged by a victim but very difficult to disprove by an accused because of the heinous nature of the crime.

—the jury should scrutinize the testimony of the victim more closely than it should scrutinize the testimony of any witness in any felony prosecution.

Pennsylvania law also provides guidelines for rape prosecutions:
- •A prompt complaint to the police regarding the attack is not required for a rape prosecution.
- •The credibility of the victim of a sexual offense shall be determined by the same standard of credibility as that applied to any other witness.
- •The victim need not resist for a prosecution for a sexual offense.

Laws Protecting Victims of Rape State-by-State

ALABAMA

Rape Shield Law: Prohibits evidence relating to the past sexual behavior of the victim, the victim's marital history, the victim's mode of dress, the victim's general reputation.

Exceptions: Evidence regarding the victim's prior sexual conduct with the defendant.

HIV Testing: There is no law in Alabama that enables the victim of a sexual assault to compel the offender to submit to testing for the AIDS virus.

ALASKA

Rape Shield Law: Prohibits evidence relating to the victim's prior sexual conduct unless the court finds that the evidence is relevant and that its probative value is not outweighed by the prejudice, confusion of the issues, or invasion of the privacy of the victim that its admission will cause.

HIV Testing: There is no law in Alaska that enables a victim of sexual assault to compel the offender to submit to testing for the AIDS virus.

ARIZONA

Rape Shield Law: Arizona does not have a specific rape shield law. However, there are rules of evidence in Arizona that prohibit evidence regarding the reputation of any witnesses, except for their reputation for truthfulness. These laws have been used as a rape shield law, to prevent the introduction of evidence regarding the victim's sexual conduct.

HIV Testing: The victim of a sexual assault may petition the court, with the prosecutor's assistance, for an order requiring that the defendant undergo testing for the AIDS virus. This procedure is available after the defendant is convicted of the sexual assault.

ARKANSAS

Rape Shield Law: Prohibits evidence relating to the victim's prior sexual conduct unless the court determines that it is relevant and not unduly prejudicial.

HIV Testing: The victim of a sexual assault may request that the offender be ordered to undergo testing for the AIDS virus. The court will order testing unless it finds that testing would be inappropriate. This procedure is available after the court has determined that there is probable cause to bind the defendant over on charges. After a conviction, testing is mandatory, upon the victim's request.

CALIFORNIA

Rape Shield Law: Prohibits evidence relating to the victim's reputation, or specific instances of the victim's sexual conduct.

Exceptions: Evidence of specific instances of the victim's sexual conduct with the defendant.

HIV Testing: A court may order that the defendant be tested for the AIDS virus, and the results disclosed to the victim if the court finds that there is probable cause to believe that there was a transfer of bodily fluid. This type of order is available before a conviction.

COLORADO

Rape Shield Law: Prohibits evidence relating to the victim's sexual conduct prior to or after the sexual assault, and the victim's reputation.

Exceptions: Evidence regarding sexual conduct with the accused, and evidence offered to explain the victim's pregnancy, the origin of a sexually transmitted disease or to explain the presence of semen on the person of the victim or her clothing.

HIV Testing: In cases involving sexual assault, the court shall order that the defendant undergo a test for HIV and that the results be disclosed to the victim. This type of order is entered after the defendant is bound over for trial.

CONNECTICUT

Rape Shield Law: Prohibits evidence relating to the victim's sexual conduct.

Exceptions: Evidence offered to show the source of semen, disease, pregnancy or injury, or evidence offered to impeach the victim's credibility if she testifies regarding her sexual conduct, or evidence regarding prior sexual activity between the defendant and the victim if the defendant claims that the victim consented to sexual activity.

HIV Testing: A court may order any person to undergo testing for the AIDS virus if another proves that he or she has a "compelling need" to know if that person is infected. This is not limited to situations involving sexual assault.

DELAWARE

Rape Shield Law: Prohibits evidence relating to the victim's reputation and the opinion that others hold of her, and evidence of specific instances of the victim's sexual conduct.

Exceptions: Evidence regarding specific instances of sexual conduct with the defendant.

HIV Testing: The court presiding over a criminal prosecution may order that the defendant be tested for the AIDS virus only if it is relevant to the ultimate issue of culpability or liability.

FLORIDA

Rape Shield Law: Prohibits evidence relating to the victim's sexual activity, the victim's reputation, and the victim's manner of dress.

Exceptions: Evidence offered to prove that the defendant is not the source of semen, pregnancy, injury or disease, and evidence relevant to the issue of consent.

HIV Testing: Upon the request of the victim of a sexual offense which involves the transmission of body fluids from one person to another, the court shall order that the defendant undergo testing for the AIDS virus. This type of order is available after charges have been filed as well as after a conviction. The results are not admissible in the trial for the sexual offense.

GEORGIA

Rape Shield Law: Prohibits evidence relating to the victim's past sexual behavior, the victim's marital history, the victim's mode of dress, and the victim's reputation.

Exceptions: Evidence of the victim's past sexual conduct with the defendant is admissible if it is relevant to the issue of consent.

HIV Testing: The court may require that any person convicted of a crime that could result in the transmission of the AIDS virus be tested, and that the test results be released to the victim.

HAWAII

Rape Shield Law: Prohibits evidence relating to the victim's reputation, and the victim's past sexual behavior.

Exceptions: Evidence offered to show that the defendant was not the source of semen or injury, and evidence of sexual behavior with the accused, offered to show consent.

HIV Testing: Hawaii law has no provision that enables a victim of sexual assault to compel the offender to submit to testing for the AIDS virus.

IDAHO

Rape Shield Law: Prohibits evidence relating to the victim's previous sexual conduct.

Exceptions: Evidence offered to show the source of semen or injury, and evidence regarding sexual conduct with the accused, offered to show consent, and evidence regarding previous false accusations of sexual crimes, and evidence regarding sexual conduct with others at the same time as the accused.

HIV Testing: Any person who is incarcerated in Idaho must be tested for the AIDS virus. If that person was convicted of a sexual crime, the test results may be released to his or her victims.

ILLINOIS

Rape Shield Law: Prohibits evidence relating to the victim's prior sexual activity, and the victim's reputation.

Exceptions: Evidence of the victim's previous sexual activity with the accused.

HIV Testing: A victim of a sexual assault may request that the prosecuting attorney apply for a court order that the accused undergo testing for the AIDS virus. The results of the testing are to be released to the court and the victim. The victim may make this request after the accused has been indicted or after he has been ordered to stand trial following a preliminary hearing.

INDIANA

Rape Shield Law: Prohibits evidence relating to the victim's past sexual conduct, and the victim's reputation or opinion evidence regarding the victim's past sexual conduct.

Exceptions: Evidence regarding the victim's sexual activity with the defendant, and evidence that tends to prove that someone else committed the sexual offense, and evidence used to prove that the victim's pregnancy is not due to the defendant.

HIV Testing: All persons who are convicted of sexual crimes shall be ordered to undergo testing for the AIDS virus. If the offender tests positive, the results are to be made available to his or her victims.

IOWA

Rape Shield Law: There is no rape shield law in Iowa that applies to criminal prosecutions. Iowa law does provide that in civil actions for damages from a sexual assault, evidence regarding the past sexual behavior of the victim is prohibited.

HIV Testing: The victim of a sexual assault may petition the court, through the prosecutor, to order the offender to undergo testing for the AIDS virus if the sexual assault created a significant risk of exposure to the virus and if the offender refuses to voluntarily undergo testing. This procedure is available after the conviction.

KANSAS

Rape Shield Law: Prohibits evidence relating to the victim's previous sexual conduct, unless the court finds that it is relevant.

HIV Testing: Upon the victim's request, the court shall order any person convicted of a crime involving the transmission of body fluids to undergo testing for the AIDS virus. If the defendant tests negative, he or she shall be tested again in six months.

KENTUCKY

Rape Shield Law: Prohibits evidence relating to the victim's reputation or opinion evidence regarding the victim's sexual behavior, and the victim's past sexual behavior.

Exceptions: Evidence regarding the victim's sexual conduct with persons other than the accused if it is offered to explain the source of injury or semen, and evidence regarding the victim's sexual conduct with the accused if it is relevant to the issue of consent.

HIV Testing: Upon a conviction for sexual assault, the offender shall be ordered to undergo testing for the AIDS virus, and the results are to be made available to the victim.

LOUISIANA

Rape Shield Law: Prohibits evidence relating to the victim's reputation or opinion evidence regarding the victim's past sexual conduct, and specific instances of the victim's sexual conduct.

Exceptions: Evidence regarding the victim's sexual conduct with others to show the accused is not the source of injury or semen, and evidence regarding the victim's sexual conduct with the accused to show consent.

HIV Testing: Persons convicted of sexual assault shall be ordered to undergo testing for the AIDS virus, and the results shall be released to the victim.

MAINE

Rape Shield Law: The state of Maine does not have a rape shield law.

HIV Testing: The victim of a sexual assault may petition the court to order that the offender undergo testing for the AIDS virus. The victim must have undergone testing within six weeks of his or her possible exposure, must have already unsuccessfully sought the offender's consent to testing, and there must have been a significant risk of HIV infection. This procedure is available after conviction.

MARYLAND

Rape Shield Law: Prohibits evidence relating to the victim's reputation, and specific instances of the victim's sexual conduct.

Exceptions: Evidence regarding the victim's past sexual conduct with the defendant, and evidence that shows the source of semen, pregnancy, disease or trauma, and evidence that shows that the victim had a motive to make a false accusation of rape.

HIV Testing: Upon the victim's request, a convicted sexual offender shall be ordered to undergo testing for the AIDS virus, if there is the possibility of exposure to the virus. An accused may be required to undergo testing prior to a conviction if the court finds that there is probable cause to believe that the victim was exposed. The results of the testing are to be made available to the victim.

MASSACHUSETTS

Rape Shield Law: Prohibits evidence relating to the victim's previous sexual conduct.

Exceptions: Evidence regarding conduct with the defendant, and evidence of recent sexual conduct that is alleged to be the cause of the victim's physical condition.

HIV Testing: Massachusetts law has no provision that enables a victim of sexual assault to compel the offender to submit to testing for the AIDS virus.

MICHIGAN

Rape Shield Law: Prohibits evidence relating to specific instances of the victim' sexual conduct, and opinion and reputation evidence regarding the victim's sexual conduct.

Exceptions: Evidence of the victim's sexual conduct with the defendant, and evidence regarding the source of semen, pregnancy or disease.

HIV Testing: Upon conviction, a sexual offender shall be tested for the AIDS virus. The testing agency may provide the results to the victim, if the victim consents to receiving the results.

MINNESOTA

Rape Shield Law: Prohibits evidence relating to the victim's previous sexual conduct.

Exceptions: Evidence relevant to the issue of consent, and evidence that establishes a common scheme or plan showing that the victim has previously fabricated allegations of sexual assault, and evidence regarding previous sexual conduct with the accused, and evidence that shows the source of semen, pregnancy or disease.

HIV Testing: Upon the victim's request, the court may order that the offender undergo testing for the AIDS virus, if there is evidence that in the course of the crime the broken skin or mucous membrane of the victim came into contact with the offender's semen or blood. The results of the test are to be made available to the victim. This procedure is available after conviction.

MISSISSIPPI

Rape Shield Law: Prohibits evidence relating to the victim's reputation or opinion evidence regarding the victim's past sexual behavior.

Exceptions: Evidence regarding the victim's past sexual conduct with others to show the source of semen, pregnancy, disease or injury, evidence regarding the victim's past sexual behavior with the defendant if relevant to the issue of consent, and evidence regarding the victim's previous false allegations of sexual offenses.

HIV Testing: Any person convicted of a sexual offense and sentenced to prison shall be tested for the AIDS virus. Any positive results shall be reported to the victim.

MISSOURI

Rape Shield Law: Prohibits evidence relating to the victim's reputation and opinions regarding the victim's prior sexual conduct.

Exceptions: Evidence of specific instances of the victim's conduct with the defendant, relevant to the issue of consent, and evidence that shows an alternative source of pregnancy, semen or disease, and evidence regarding the immediate circumstances of the crime, and evidence regarding the victim's previous sexual conduct if the victim's previous chastity is a necessary element of the crime and the evidence shows that the victim was unchaste.

HIV Testing: All persons who are committed to the Missouri Department of Corrections must be tested for the AIDS virus. The Department shall inform the victims of sexual offenders of the test results.

MONTANA

Rape Shield Law: Prohibits evidence relating to the victim's sexual conduct.

Exceptions: Evidence regarding the victim's sexual conduct with the accused, and evidence offered to show the origin of semen, pregnancy or disease.

HIV Testing: At the victim's request, a person convicted of a sexual offense must undergo testing for the AIDS virus, and the results must be made available to the victim.

NEBRASKA

Rape Shield Law: Prohibits evidence relating to the victim's past sexual behavior.

Exceptions: Evidence that shows the source of any physical evidence (semen, injury, blood, saliva, hair), and evidence regarding sexual behavior with the defendant if it tends to prove consent.

HIV Testing: At the victim's request, the court shall order a convicted sexual offender to undergo testing for the AIDS virus.

NEVADA

Rape Shield Law: Prohibits evidence relating to the victim's previous sexual conduct.

Exceptions: In the event the prosecutor has introduced evidence regarding the victim's previous conduct or the victim has testified regarding her conduct or lack of conduct. Such evidence may be admitted if it is relevant to the issue of consent.

HIV Testing: The defendant in a sexual assault case must be tested for the AIDS virus upon his or her arrest. The results of the testing must be provided to the victim.

NEW HAMPSHIRE

Rape Shield Law: Prohibits evidence relating to the victim's prior sexual activity with anyone other than the defendant.

HIV Testing: The victim of a sexual assault may request that the State administer an AIDS test and release the results to her, after the offender's conviction.

NEW JERSEY

Rape Shield Law: Prohibits evidence relating to the victim's previous sexual conduct unless the court finds that the evidence is relevant, and that its probative value is not outweighed by prejudice, confusion of the issues or invasion of the victim's privacy.

HIV Testing: New Jersey law has no provision that enables a victim of sexual assault to compel the offender to submit to testing for the AIDS virus.

NEW MEXICO

Rape Shield Law: Prohibits evidence relating to the victim's past sexual conduct, and the victim's reputation or opinion evidence regarding the victim's past sexual conduct, unless such evidence is relevant to the issues and its prejudicial nature does not outweigh its probative value.

HIV Testing: New Mexico law has no provision that enables a victim of sexual assault to compel the offender to submit to testing for the AIDS virus.

NEW YORK

Rape Shield Law: Prohibits evidence relating to the victim's sexual conduct.

Exceptions: Evidence that proves specific instances of prior conduct with the accused, and evidence that proves that the victim was convicted of prostitution within three years, and evidence that rebuts or refutes evidence that the victim had not engaged in intercourse during a certain time, and evidence that rebuts or refutes evidence that the accused is the source or cause of pregnancy, disease or semen.

HIV Testing: New York law has no provision that enables a victim of sexual assault to compel an offender to submit to testing for the AIDS virus. However, courts may order disclosure of AIDS re-

131

lated information upon a showing that there is a "compelling need for disclosure of information for the adjudication of a criminal or civil proceeding."

NORTH CAROLINA

Rape Shield Law: Prohibits evidence relating to the victim's past sexual behavior.

Exceptions: Evidence regarding sexual behavior with the defendant, and evidence that shows that the acts charged were not committed by the defendant, and evidence of sexual conduct with another "... of a pattern of sexual behavior so distinctive and so closely resembling the defendant's version of the alleged encounter with the complainant as to tend to prove that such complainant consented to the act or acts charged or behaved in such a manner as to lead the defendant reasonably to believe that the complainant consented." and evidence offered as the basis of an expert opinion that the complainant invented the act charged.

HIV Testing: The victim of a sexual offense may request that the prosecutor petition the court to order that the offender be tested for the AIDS virus. There must be probable cause to find that the alleged sexual conduct would pose a significant risk of transmission.

NORTH DAKOTA

Rape Shield Law: Prohibits evidence relating to the victim's mode of dress, unless it is relevant and its inflammatory nature does not outweigh its probative value, and the victim's reputation or opinion evidence regarding the victim, and evidence of specific instances of the victim's sexual conduct.

Exceptions: Evidence regarding sexual conduct with the defendant which tends to prove consent.

HIV Testing: Upon the victim's request, the court may order a defendant charged with a sexual offense to undergo testing for the AIDS virus. The court must first find that there is probable cause to believe that a transfer of body fluids took place.

OHIO

Rape Shield Law: Prohibits evidence relating to specific instances of the victim's sexual conduct, and the victim's reputation and opinion evidence regarding the victim's sexual conduct.

Exceptions: Evidence that shows the origin of semen, pregnancy or disease, and evidence of the victim's sexual conduct with the accused.

HIV Testing: The court shall order any person charged with a sexual offense to be tested for the AIDS virus. The court shall then inform the victim that the test was performed and that the victim has the right to know the results.

OKLAHOMA

Rape Shield Law: Prohibits evidence relating to the victim's reputation and opinion evidence regarding the victim's sexual behavior and the victim's sexual behavior with anyone other than the accused.

Exceptions: Evidence that shows the source of semen, pregnancy, disease or injury, and evidence of previous false allegations of sexual assault, and evidence that shows that similar acts were performed in the presence of the accused at the same time as the alleged sexual assault.

HIV Testing: Upon the arraignment of any person charged with sexual assault, the Court shall order the accused to undergo testing for the AIDS virus. The victim is entitled to notification of the test results.

OREGON

Rape Shield Law: Prohibits evidence relating to the victim's reputation or opinion evidence regarding the victim's past sexual conduct, and the victim's past sexual behavior.

Exceptions: Evidence that relates to the motive or bias of the victim, and evidence necessary to rebut or explain scientific or medical evidence offered by the state.

HIV Testing: At the victim's request, if the crime was one in which transmission of body fluids was likely to be involved, the court may order the offender to submit to testing for the AIDs virus, if the victim has submitted to such testing. The court may order a subsequent HIV test six months later, if the first test is negative. This procedure is available after the conviction.

PENNSYLVANIA

Rape Shield Law: Prohibits evidence relating to specific instances of the victim's past sexual conduct, and the victim's reputation and opinion evidence regarding her past sexual conduct.

Exceptions: Evidence of the victim's sexual conduct with the accused offered to prove consent.

HIV Testing: Pennsylvania law has no provision that enables the victim of a sexual assault to compel the offender to submit to testing for the AIDS virus. However, any individual may apply for an order for testing for the AIDS virus, and disclosure of test results if that individual was exposed to the body fluid of the person for whom testing is sought and the exposure presents a significant risk of exposure to HIV infection.

RHODE ISLAND

Rape Shield Law: Rhode Island law does not prohibit the introduction of evidence regarding the victim's sexual activities with other persons, but the court has the right to rule on the admissibility of such evidence outside the hearing of the jury.

HIV Testing: Rhode Island law has no provision that enables the victim of sexual assault to compel the offender to submit to testing for the AIDS virus. All inmates entering the correctional system are tested, as are all persons convicted of prostitution and IV drug offenses, but there are no provisions for the release of test results to the victims of their crimes.

SOUTH CAROLINA

Rape Shield Law: Prohibits evidence relating to specific instances of the victim's sexual conduct, and the victim's reputation and opinion evidence of the victim's sexual conduct.

Exceptions: Evidence regarding the victim's conduct with the defendant or others may be introduced to show the source or origin of semen, pregnancy or disease, and evidence of specific instances of sexual activity which would constitute adultery are admissible to impeach the credibility of the witness.

HIV Testing: Within 15 days of conviction for a sexual offense, if the crime resulted in the exposure of the victim to blood or vaginal or seminal fluids of the offender, the offender shall be tested for the AIDS virus, and the results released to the victim.

SOUTH DAKOTA

Rape Shield Law: Prohibits evidence relating to specific instances of the victim's prior sexual conduct, unless the court determines that it is relevant and material.

HIV Testing: The victim of a violent sexual assault may request that the prosecutor obtain a search warrant to test the blood of the defendant for the AIDS virus, if there was an exchange of blood, semen or bodily fluids. The victim is entitled to notice of the results, but the results may not be used to establish the defendant's guilt or innocence.

TENNESSEE

Rape Shield Law: Prohibits evidence relating to specific instances of the victim's sexual behavior, and the victim's reputation or opinion evidence of the victim's sexual behavior.

Exceptions: Evidence offered to rebut evidence offered by the prosecution, and evidence of the victim's behavior with the accused, if relevant to the issue of consent, and evidence of conduct with others, offered to rebut or explain scientific or medical evidence or to explain the source of semen, injury, disease or knowledge of sexual matters, and evidence of a pattern of sexual behavior so distinctive and so closely resembling the accused's version of the alleged encounter with the victim that it tends to prove that the victim consented or behaved in such a manner as to lead the defendant reasonably to believe that the victim consented.

TEXAS

Rape Shield Law: Prohibits evidence relating to the victim's reputation or opinion evidence regarding the victim's sexual conduct, and specific instances of the victim's sexual conduct.

Exceptions: Evidence necessary to rebut or explain scientific or medical evidence offered by the state, and evidence of sexual conduct with the accused, offered to show consent, and evidence of the victim's motive or bias.

HIV Testing: Persons indicted for sexual offenses shall be tested for the AIDS virus on the motion of the victim or the court's own motion. The test results are to be made available to the victim.

UTAH

Rape Shield Law: The state of Utah has no rape shield law.

HIV Testing: Upon the request of the victim, a person convicted of a sexual offense or attempted sexual offense must submit to testing for the AIDS virus. The results are to be made available to the victim.

VERMONT

Rape Shield Law: Prohibits evidence relating to the victim's reputation and opinion evidence regarding the victim's sexual conduct, and specific instances of the victim's prior sexual conduct.

Exceptions: Evidence of the victim's past sexual conduct with the defendant, if it bears on the issue of credibility, and evidence that shows the source or origin of pregnancy, injury and disease, and evidence of past false allegations of sexual assault.

HIV Testing: Vermont has no law that allows the victim of a sexual assault to compel the offender to submit to testing for the AIDS virus. If the offender has been tested, the victim may get an order compelling the disclosure of the results, if the victim can demonstrate a compelling need for such disclosure.

VIRGINIA

Rape Shield Law: Prohibits evidence relating to the victim's reputation or opinion evidence regarding the victim's prior sexual conduct, and specific instances of the victim's prior sexual conduct.

Exceptions: Evidence offered to provide an alternative explanation for physical evidence presented by the prosecution or designed to explain the presence of semen, pregnancy, disease or injury, and evidence regarding sexual conduct with the accused to support a contention that the sexual act complained of was consensual.

HIV Testing: Upon a finding of probable cause that the accused committed a sexual offense, the Court shall order the accused to undergo testing for the AIDS virus. The offender may also be ordered to undergo testing upon conviction. The results shall be disclosed to the victim. The results may not be used in the criminal prosecution.

WASHINGTON

Rape Shield Law: Prohibits evidence relating to the victim's past sexual history, including marital history and divorce history, and the victim's general reputation.

Exceptions: Evidence regarding the victim's past sexual behavior with the defendant, if relevant to the issue of consent.

HIV Testing: All persons convicted of sexual offenses must be ordered, at sentencing, to undergo testing for the AIDS virus. A victim may obtain access to the results by a court order, upon a showing of good cause.

WEST VIRGINIA

Rape Shield Law: Prohibits evidence relating to specific instances of the victim's sexual conduct, and the victim's reputation and opinion evidence regarding the victim's sexual conduct.

Exceptions: Evidence regarding the victim's past sexual conduct with the defendant, if relevant to the issue of consent, and evidence regarding the victim's sexual conduct with others, but only to impeach her credibility if she first introduces evidence regarding prior sexual conduct.

HIV Testing: The court shall order testing for the AIDS virus be performed on any person convicted of a sexual offense. The results are to be made available to the victim.

WISCONSIN

Rape Shield Law: Prohibits evidence relating to the victim's past sexual conduct, and the victim's reputation and opinion evidence regarding the victim's past sexual conduct.

Exceptions: Evidence regarding conduct with the accused, and evidence showing the source or origin of semen, pregnancy or disease, and evidence of prior untruthful allegations of sexual assault made by the victim.

HIV Testing: Upon the request of the victim, the prosecutor may apply for an order that the accused undergo testing for the AIDS virus if there is probable cause to believe the defendant has exposed the victim to the virus. The results are to be made available to the victim.

137

WYOMING

Rape Shield Law: Wyoming law does not bar the admission of the victim's prior sexual conduct, reputation evidence or opinion evidence if, after a hearing, the court finds that the probative value of the evidence substantially outweighs the probability that its admission will create prejudice.

HIV Testing: All inmates entering the Wyoming Correctional system are tested for sexually transmitted diseases, but there are no provisions in Wyoming law that enable victims of sexual assault to compel the offender to submit to testing for the AIDS virus or to gain access to the results.

CHAPTER 8

VICTIMS OF DOMESTIC VIOLENCE

Barbara and Jim had been dating for seven months and were considering marriage when they decided to rent an apartment together. Barbara knew that Jim had a bad temper, but he had never been abusive towards her.

After a month of living together, Barbara discovered that she was pregnant. Jim had told her that he didn't want children, and he became enraged when she told him about the pregnancy. He accused her of having deliberately set out to "trap" him, then punched her in the face and stormed out of their apartment.

The next day he came home and was full of remorse when he saw her swollen black eye. He brought her flowers and they started making plans to get married before the baby arrived. For a few days, they happily contemplated their future as a family.

However, within a week, Jim started going to "happy hour" after work. He told Barbara he wanted to enjoy his freedom before the baby came. "Happy hour" seemed to last longer every night, and one night Jim didn't come home at all. When he did return the next day, Barbara and Jim had a violent argument. Jim pushed Barbara against a wall, and she locked herself in the bedroom.

Then Barbara noticed blood in her underpants. She called to Jim for help, fearing that she might be having a miscarriage. Jim was as frightened as she was, and he rushed her to the hospital. The doctors kept Barbara overnight for observation, and then released her, when it appeared that the pregnancy was not in danger.

Jim took Barbara home, and was more attentive than ever. For a while, it appeared that they would be able to work out their problems.

In her seventh month of pregnancy, Barbara developed high blood pressure. Her doctor advised her that she would have to leave her job and stay off her feet until the baby was born. With the loss of Barbara's income, things became very stressful at home. Once again, Jim began spending his evenings in bars. Barbara only complained once about his absences. When she did, Jim threatened to kick her in the stomach "So she could get back to work."

When their child was born, Jim wasn't at the hospital. He did pick Barbara up when she was ready for release, but showed no interest in their baby. He only displayed intense resentment at his new responsibilities, and irritation at the baby's crying and constant need for Barbara's attention.

One night, Jim came home drunk. The baby had been colicky all day, and Barbara was at her wit's end. Jim told her to "shut the brat up," and Barbara began to cry. She asked Jim why he couldn't act like a father. In response, Jim slapped her, then threw her to the floor and kicked her several times. He choked her until she passed out.

When she regained consciousness, Jim was gone, and her baby was crying. Unable to stand because of the sharp pain in her side, she crawled to the phone and dialed 911. The police and Emergency Medical Technicians arrived minutes later.

Barbara told the police officers what happened. They advised her that they would find and arrest Jim. Barbara is still afraid of Jim, and of what will happen if she presses charges. Because of this, she isn't sure that she wants Jim to be prosecuted. Can the police arrest Jim if she refuses to sign a complaint?

Yes. Almost every state has a law that allows the police to arrest, without a warrant, any person whom they suspect of having committed an act of domestic violence. These laws have been enacted because many victims of domestic violence are simply not emotionally able to take on the responsibility of pressing a criminal complaint. This allows the police to initiate the proceedings on their own. The decision to arrest is not dependent on the victim's consent or request. In some states, such as Connecticut, there are now laws that make it mandatory for the police to make an arrest for family violence crimes. In states without such a law, many local police departments have a mandatory arrest policy.

Barbara feels safe for the time being, but she knows that after Jim is arrested, he'll make bail and be back at their apartment,

madder than ever. Barbara and her child have nowhere to go. Is there any protection available for her while she's waiting for Jim to go to court?

Yes. In some states, after an arrest for domestic violence, the court can place conditions on the offender's release on bail. The court can require that the defendant refrain from harassing or contacting the victim. The court can require that the defendant vacate the family home. If appropriate, the court can require that the defendant attend counseling, or refrain from the use of drugs or alcohol. In some states, such as Ohio and Illinois, the law allows the court to enter an Order of Protection in conjunction with the criminal case. Orders of Protection are discussed at length later in this chapter.

In states without laws that specifically address bail in instances of family violence, the court may still use its discretionary power to impose conditions on the defendant's bail, and enter orders prohibiting the defendant from contacting the victim.

How can Barbara find out what rights she has and what services are available to her from the state?

Some states require that their peace officers inform victims of domestic violence of their rights and the services that are available to them. For example, Alaska law provides that when responding to a call involving domestic violence, law enforcement officers must inform the victim that he or she:

> 1. May seek the aid and shelter of an organization designed to protect the victims of domestic violence. The officer must provide the address of the nearest shelter.
> 2. Should tell the officer if he or she still feels in danger, and the officer will take steps to insure the victim's safety.
> 3. May obtain an order of protection, and an attorney is not necessary.
> 4. May contact the victim/witness assistance program at the prosecutor's office.

California's Penal Code provides that peace officers should:

1. Assist the victim in pursuing a criminal prosecution by giving him or her the police report number and directing the victim to the proper investigative unit.

2. Warn the victim that the abuser could be released and provide the victim with information regarding shelters and other services available to victims of domestic violence.

3. Advise the victim that he or she may request that the District Attorney file a criminal complaint against the abuser.

4. Advise the victim that he or she may file a petition for a civil order of protection.

5. Advise the victim that her or she may file a civil lawsuit against the abuser to recover for losses suffered due to the abuse.

6. In cases where there has been a sexual assault, advise the victim of the locations of rape victim counseling centers, the proper procedures for a victim to follow after a rape, and advise the victim that acquaintance rape and spousal rape are crimes.

If Barbara changes her mind about a criminal prosecution, can the DA force her to testify against Jim?

Yes, in most cases. A criminal proceeding is a case brought by the state, not by an individual. This means that a crime victim does not control the prosecution. The victim cannot require that a prosecution be commenced, nor can a victim compel the state to abandon a prosecution. If Barbara refuses to testify, the court could hold her in contempt.

Because it is often difficult for victims of domestic violence to assist in the prosecution of their abusers, California law provides that the court may not hold a victim of domestic violence in contempt for refusing to testify. However, the court may require the victim to attend up to 72 hours of education regarding domestic violence.

Jim has a clean record. Barbara suspects that even if he's convicted of the attack on her, he'll receive probation. Is there anything that she can do?

Many victims of family or domestic violence have suffered many beatings or other types of violence before a case is actually prosecuted. If the abuser is convicted of a simple case of battery based on one incident, the judge who will be handing down a sentence against him may not understand that the one incident that is before the court is only one in a long series. The judge may be inclined to impose a suspended sentence or probation, when a jail sentence might actually be more appropriate. In such a case the victim should tell the prosecutor, prior to any sentencing hearing, about the full history of the relationship, supplying corroborating photographs, medical records or witnesses, if available. This information can then be presented to the judge, so that he or she understands that the abuser has engaged in a continuing pattern of violence, and is dangerous.

The state of Florida has a law which requires that police officers who respond to a report of domestic violence file a report, even if an arrest is not made. In a state with such a law, or in a town where the police have such a policy, the victim of domestic abuse may be able to present police records of previous incidents of violence.

If the court is likely to grant probation, Barbara should consult with the prosecutor, and request that the prosecutor recommend that Jim participate in counseling.

Barbara is certain that she does not want to prosecute Jim in th criminal courts. She doesn't want to put her child's father in jail, and frankly, she is in desperate need of his financial support. However, she recognizes that Jim is becoming more and more violent toward her. Is there anything she can do to protect herself, without going through a criminal prosecution?

Yes. Almost every state has civil laws designed to protect the victims of domestic violence. Domestic violence is usually defined as threats of immediate harm, or actual acts of violence against a spouse, a former spouse, a parent, child, grandparent, grandchild, a housemate who is in the home in a dating, courtship or engagement relationship, or persons not living together who have children together. It is usually not applied in roommate situations, where there is no family or intimate relationship. The definition of domestic violence is not limited to actual physical harm or threats of physical harm under all laws. For example:

- •Hawaii law includes extreme psychological abuse and malicious property damage in its definition of domestic violence.
- •Idaho law includes forced imprisonment in its definition of domestic violence.
- •Illinois law prohibits harassment such as creating a disturbance at school or work, repeated phone calls, keeping another under surveillance and concealing or threatening to conceal the victim's child.
- •Massachusetts law includes forcible sexual relations in its definition of abuse.

Under these laws, a person who has been threatened with, or been the victim of domestic abuse may file a civil petition requesting the court's protection. If appropriate the court will issue an order of protection or a restraining order against the perpetrator of the violence.

Does Barbara need a lawyer to file a petition?

No, a lawyer is not necessary. However, a party filing a petition for an order of protection has the right to retain a lawyer to assist him or her with the legal process. In some areas, the court, the prosecutor's office, local law enforcement, or shelters for the victims of domestic violence provide advocates who can assist in the process. In other areas legal aid societies provide lawyers for persons filing petitions. Most courts provide fairly simple forms and an informal and expedited procedure, so that legal representation isn't absolutely necessary.

Any person considering filing a petition without the assistance of an attorney should consider that when a hearing is scheduled, the abuser may appear with an attorney. The victim of domestic violence should seriously consider having the assistance of counsel at the hearing.

What information will Barbara need to provide to the court?

When filing a petition, the plaintiff or petitioner should be prepared to detail the injury, or the threats that he or she has suffered. The court will also need to know if the petitioner has children with the abuser, if he or she is in need of child support or spousal support, and if the petitioner needs exclusive possession of the family home. The petitioner should also inform the court if a place of employment or school should be covered by the order of protection, and if there is an immediate threat of danger. The court may also request a physical description or photograph of the respondent, and information regarding his or her address, place of employment, and any alias he or she might use.

If child custody is an issue, the petitioner should be prepared to provide the court with information regarding where the children have lived, and with whom the children have lived for the preceding five years. The petitioner must also provide the court with information regarding any child custody proceedings in the past, or currently pending, involving the children. If requesting child support, the petitioner should know the respondent's income, and be prepared to give the court child care costs, medical costs and the costs of health insurance.

If there is an action already pending between the parties, such as a paternity and support action, or a divorce case, the petitioner should give the court details regarding that other legal proceeding and supply the court with copies of any orders generated by those proceedings.

Although Barbara convinced the prosecutor to not go forward in criminal court, Jim spent a night in jail. When he got out he called Barbara at the hospital and threatened her. When Barbara files her petition, the hearing won't be held for at least a week. Will she be without protection until the hearing?

No. Under the domestic violence laws, the courts have the authority to grant temporary orders of protection on the spot, without notice to the defendant or the respondent. This type of hearing, where only one of the parties is present, is called an *ex parte* hearing. The court will also set a date for a full hearing, to hear both sides of the case and to determine if the temporary order should be extended. The petitioner should be sure to appear at the full hearing, or the order of protection will be terminated.

If the court grants a petition for a civil order of protection, it can enter a wide variety of orders designed to protect the victim from further violence.

The cornerstone of a civil order of protection is the restraining order. Typically, this portion of the order prohibits the defendant or respondent from coming into contact with his or her victim. If the parties share a home, the respondent is ordered to vacate the residence. The court may further order that the respondent stay away from the victim's place of business, employment, or his or her school. The respondent is directed to refrain from contacting, telephoning, harassing, molesting or further abusing the victim. Restraining orders may extend to protect the petitioner's children, and in New Hampshire, the court may enjoin the respondent from harassing the petitioner's relatives. In Massachusetts, the order may prohibit the respondent from damaging the petitioner's property or shutting off the petitioner's mail or utilities.

If the parties have children together, then the court must make provision for their custody and for contact with the non-custodial parent. In most cases, custody of the children will be awarded to the petitioner, not to the abuser. The court must then make orders for visitation. If necessary, the court may prohibit contact between the respondent and the children, or direct that visitation take place under supervision.

Parents have a duty to support their children, even if one parent has been ordered out of the family home. When making provisions for child custody and visitation, the court may also enter an order that the respondent pay child support on a regular basis. If the respondent also owes the petitioner a duty of support, (for example, if they are married), the court may enter an order for spousal support as well. If there is a duty to support, and the respondent is the sole owner of the family residence, the court might order the respondent to provide suitable alternative housing for the petitioner and children.

Some state laws allow the court to direct that the parties, or only the respondent, engage in counseling. The court may be able to order the respondent to reimburse the petitioner for damages, medical bills, counseling fees or attorneys fees. Some states grant the courts the power to order that the respondent turn over jointly owned items of personal property, such as automobiles, to the petitioner for his or her use. The court may grant the respondent the right to make one visit to the family home, to retrieve personal belongings, under the supervision of law enforcement officers.

Barbara received an order of protection, and the court directed Jim to vacate their apartment. The court also entered a child support order. As she was leaving the courthouse, Jim said to her "It's only a piece of paper." What can Barbara do if Jim threatens her again, or if he refuses to pay the child support?

Violations of an order of protection may be punished as contempt of court. For wilful contempt of court, the court may impose a fine, or even send the offender to jail. In addition, many states make violation of an order of protection a misdemeanor which is punishable by a fine or imprisonment. In these cases the penalties may be fines up to $1,000 and imprisonment for up to one year.

Some states also provide that subsequent violations incur harsher punishment and mandatory jail time. For example, in Missouri, a violation may be punished as a Class A misdemeanor, or a Class D felony, depending on the history of violations and the severity of the violation. Along similar lines, in Illinois, if the violation is in the nature of a trespass, it is treated as a misdemeanor, while if it is in the nature of interference with a parties' custody rights, it is treated as a felony. In New Jersey, a second contempt citation results in a mandatory jail sentence of at least 30 days, and in New Mexico a second violation results in a mandatory 72 hours in jail, at the very least.

Contempt citations and misdemeanor prosecutions are useful for non-violent violations of the court order, such as failure to provide support, or telephoning the petitioner after being ordered not to. Sometimes, however, the violation comes in the form of a violent confrontation, malicious destruction of property, stalking, or breaking and entering. In those cases, the respondent may be prosecuted for the underlying crime, as well as for wilful violation of an order of protection.

147

Barbara's order will expire in a year. During that year, Jim is not allowed to come to her apartment. If he goes to counseling, and both of them want to try to make their relationship work again, can the order be changed before the year is up?

Yes. Orders of protection may be modified or dissolved before their expiration. In most cases, a party seeking to modify the order must file a motion and present evidence in court. However, Barbara should consider a modification or dissolution of the order very carefully. If things don't work out and Jim becomes violent again, Barbara might not be able to get another order, as some states limit the number of orders that may be granted between particular parties in a year.

For Your Protection

Keep a copy of your order of protection, as this will assist law enforcement in the event that you report a violation of the order.

Make sure that your local police or sheriff's department has a copy of the order on file. Many domestic abuse laws require that the order be filed with law enforcement agencies, but you can better protect yourself by taking whatever steps are necessary to be sure that the law is obeyed.

Orders of Protection State-by-State

ALABAMA

The Law: Code of Alabama Sections 30-5-1 through 30-5-11.

Where to File: In the Circuit Court, or in the Superior Court if a Circuit Judge is not available.

Temporary Ex Parte Orders: Yes. A full hearing must be held within ten days.

Length of Validity: Up to one year.

Enforcement: Violations may be punished as contempt of court.

ALASKA

The Law: Alaska Statutes Section 12.61.020.

Where to File: In the Superior or District Court.

Temporary Ex Parte Orders: Yes. They are valid for up to 20 days; a full hearing is held after ten days notice to the respondent.

Length of Validity: Up to 90 days, extensions of an additional 45 days are available.

Enforcement: Violations may be punished as misdemeanors.

ARIZONA

The Law: Arizona Statutes Section 13-3602.

Where to File: With a magistrate, justice of the peace, or superior court judge.

Temporary Ex Parte Orders: Yes. A full hearing must be held within ten days of the application.

Length of Validity: Up to six months, then may be renewed.

Enforcement: Violations may be punished as crimes, or as contempt of court.

ARKANSAS

The Law: Arkansas Code Sections 9-15-101 through 9-15-211.

Where to File: In Chancery Court.

Temporary Ex Parte Orders: Yes. A full hearing must be held within 14 days.

Length of Validity: 90 days to one year, and may be extended.

Enforcement: Violations may be punished as misdemeanors or as contempt of court.

CALIFORNIA

The Law: California Family Code Section 5500 through 5807.

Where to File: In Superior Court.

Temporary Ex Parte Orders: Yes. The temporary order expires at the time set for the full hearing. This time is indicated on the order.

Length of Validity: Up to three years.

Enforcement: Violations may be punished as misdemeanors.

COLORADO

The Law: Colorado Revised Statutes Section 14-4-101 through 14-4-105.

Where to File: In District Court, County Court or Municipal Court.

Temporary Ex Parte Orders: Yes. The full hearing must be held within 14 days.

Length of Validity: Until the parties are divorced, or orders are entered in a proceeding pursuant to the Children's Code.

Enforcement: Violations may be punished as contempt of court or as misdemeanors.

CONNECTICUT

The Law: Connecticut General Statutes Section 46b-15.

Where to File: In Superior Court.

Temporary Ex Parte Orders: Yes. A full hearing must be held within 14 days.

Length of Validity: Up to 90 days, then may be extended.

Enforcement: Violations may be punished as misdemeanors or as contempt of court.

DELAWARE

The state of Delaware has no specific law providing for civil orders of protection for victims of domestic abuse.

DISTRICT OF COLUMBIA

The Law: District of Columbia Code Section 16-1001 through 16-1006.

Where to File: In the Family Division.

Temporary Ex Parte Orders: Yes. A full hearing must be held within 14 days.

Length of Validity: Up to one year.

Enforcement: Violations may be punished as contempt of court.

FLORIDA

The Law: Florida Statutes Section 741.29 through 741.31.

Where to File: In Circuit Court.

Temporary Ex Parte Orders: Yes. A full hearing must be held within 30 days.

Length of Validity: Up to one year, then may be extended.

Enforcement: Violations may be punished as contempt of court, and also as misdemeanors.

GEORGIA

The Law: Code of Georgia Section 19-13-1 through 19-13-6.

Where to File: In Superior Court.

Temporary Ex Parte Orders: Yes. A full hearing must be held within ten days.

Length of Validity: Up to six months.

Enforcement: Violations may be punished as contempt of court and as misdemeanors.

HAWAII

The Law: Hawaii Revised Statutes Section 586-1 through 586-11.

Where to File: In Family Court.

Temporary Ex Parte Orders: Yes. A full hearing must be held within 15 days.

Validity: Up to three years.

Enforcement: Violations may be punished as contempt of court or as misdemeanors.

IDAHO

The Law: Idaho Code Sections 39-6301 through 39-6317.

Where to File: In the Magistrate's Division of the District Court.

Temporary Ex Parte Orders: Yes. A full hearing must be held within 14 days.

Length of Validity: Up to three months, then renewable for up to one year.

Enforcement: Violations may be punished as misdemeanors.

ILLINOIS

The Law: 750 Illinois Compiled Statutes Section 60/101 through 60/401.

Where to File: In Circuit Court.

Temporary Ex Parte Orders: Yes. A full hearing must be held within 14 to 21 days.

Enforcement: Violations may be punished as contempt of court, misdemeanors, or felonies.

INDIANA

The Law: Indiana Statutes Title 34, Section 4-5.1-1 through 4-5.1-7.

Where to File: In any court of record.

Temporary Ex Parte Orders: Yes. They expire when the full hearing is scheduled, or at the end of 20 days, whichever occurs first.

Validity: Up to one year, or when a petition for dissolution of marriage or legal separation is filed, whichever occurs first. May be renewed for another year.

Enforcement: Violations may be punished as contempt of court.

IOWA

The Law: Iowa Code Section 236.1 through 236.18.

Where to File: In District Court.

Temporary Ex Parte Orders: Yes. A full hearing must be held within ten days.

Validity: Up to one year.

Enforcement: Violations may be punished as contempt of court.

KANSAS

The Law: Kansas Statutes Section 60-3103 through 60-3111.

Where to File: In District Court.

Temporary Ex Parte Orders: Yes. A full hearing must be held within 20 days.

Length of Validity: Up to one year, may be extended for a second year.

Enforcement: Violations may be punished as contempt of court, criminal trespass or assault.

KENTUCKY

The Law: Kentucky Revised Statutes Section 403.715 through 403.785.

Where to File: In District Court.

Temporary Ex Parte Orders: Yes. A full hearing must be held within 14 days.

Validity: Up to one year, and then may be reissued on an annual basis.

Enforcement: Violations may be punished as contempt of court and as misdemeanors.

LOUISIANA

The Law: Louisiana Statutes Section 46:2131 through 46:2142.

Where to File: In any court with jurisdiction over family or juvenile matters.

Temporary Ex Parte Orders: Yes. A full hearing must be held within ten days.

Validity: Up to three months, and then may be extended.

Enforcement: Violations may be punished as contempt of court.

MAINE

The Law: Maine Revised Statutes Title 30A Section 288.

Where to File: In District Court or Superior Court if the District Judge is not available.

Temporary Ex Parte Orders: Yes. A full hearing must be held within 21 days.

Validity: Up to one year, and then may be extended.

Enforcement: Violations may be punished as contempt of court or as Class D crimes.

MARYLAND

The Law: Code of Maryland FL Section 4-501.

Where to File: In District or Circuit Court.

Temporary Ex Parte Orders: Yes. A full hearing must be held within seven days.

Validity: Up to 200 days.

Enforcement: Violations may be punished as contempt of court and as misdemeanors.

MASSACHUSETTS

The Law: Massachusetts General Laws Chapter 209A Sections 1 through 9.

Where to File: In Superior Court, Boston Municipal Court, Probate Court, Family Court, or District Court.

Temporary Ex Parte Orders: Yes. A full hearing must be held within ten days.

Validity: Up to one year, then may be extended.

Enforcement: Violations are considered a criminal offense.

MICHIGAN

The Law: Michigan Compiled Laws Section 600.2950.

Where to File: Circuit Court.

Validity: For the period of time stated in the order.

Enforcement: Violations are treated as criminal contempt.

MINNESOTA

The Law: Minnesota Statutes Section 518B.01.

Where to File: In the court having jurisdiction over dissolution of marriage actions.

Temporary Ex Parte Orders: Yes. A full hearing must be held within 14 days.

Validity: Up to one year, unless the court finds that a longer fixed period is necessary.

Enforcement: Violations may be punished as contempt of court or as misdemeanors. The defendant may also be required to put up a bond of up to $10,000.00 to deter further violations.

MISSISSIPPI

The Law: Mississippi Code Section 93-21-1 through 93-21-29.

Where to File: In Chancery Court, or Justice Court or County Court if the Chancery judge is unavailable.

Temporary Ex Parte Orders: Yes. A full hearing must be held within ten days.

Validity: Up to one year.

Enforcement: Violations may be punished as contempt of court.

MISSOURI

The Law: Missouri Statutes Section 455.010 through 455.538.

Where to File: In Circuit or Associate Circuit Court.

Temporary Ex Parte Orders: Yes. A full hearing must be held within 15 days.

Length of Validity: Up to 180 days, and then may be extended for an additional 180 days.

Enforcement: Violations may be punished as contempt of court or as Class A misdemeanors or Class D felonies, depending on the history of violations and the severity of violations.

MONTANA

The Law: Montana Code Section 40-4-121.

Where to File: Justice Court.

Temporary Ex Parte Orders: Yes. A full hearing must be held within 20 days.

Validity: Up to one year.

Enforcement: Violations are considered a criminal offense.

NEBRASKA

The Law: Revised Statutes of Nebraska Section 42-901 through 42-929.

Where to File: In District Court or Conciliation Court

Temporary Ex Parte Orders: Yes. A full hearing must be held within 14 days.

Length of Validity: Up to one year.

Enforcement: Violations may be punished as contempt of court and as Class II misdemeanors.

NEVADA

The Law: Nevada Revised Statutes Section 33.017 through 33.100.

Where to File: In District Court.

Temporary Ex Parte Orders: Yes. They are valid for 30 days, or until the full hearing is held.

Length of Validity: Up to one year.

Enforcement: Violations may be punished as contempt of court and as misdemeanors.

NEW HAMPSHIRE

The Law: New Hampshire Revised Statutes Section 173-B:1 through 173-B:11A.

Where to File: In District Court or Superior Court.

Temporary Ex Parte Orders: Yes. A full hearing must be held within five days of the respondent's request for a hearing.

Length of Validity: Up to one year, then may be extended.

Enforcement: Violations may be punished as contempt of court.

NEW JERSEY

The Law: New Jersey Statutes Section 2C:25-18 through 2C:25-33.

Where to File: In the Family Part of Chancery Division of Superior Court.

Temporary Ex Parte Orders: Yes. A full hearing must be held within 10 days.

Length of Validity: Until dissolved or modified.

Enforcement: Violations may be punished as contempt of court.

NEW MEXICO

The Law: New Mexico Statutes Section 40-13-1 through 40-13-8.

File In District Court.

Temporary Ex Parte Orders: Yes. A full hearing must be held within ten days.

Validity: Up to six months and then may be extended for an additional six months.

Enforcement: Violations may be punished as misdemeanors.

NEW YORK

The Law: Family Court Act Sections 821-828 and 842.

Where to File: Family Court

Temporary Ex Parte Orders: Yes.

Validity: Up to one year.

Enforcement: Violations may result in revocation of probation or modification of the conditions of probation.

NORTH CAROLINA

The Law: North Carolina General Statutes Section 50 B-1 through 50B-8.

Where to File: In the District Court Division of the General Court of Justice.

Temporary Ex Parte Orders: Yes. A full hearing must be held within ten days.

Validity: Up to one year.

Enforcement: Violations may be punished as contempt of court.

NORTH DAKOTA

The Law: North Dakota Century Code Sections 14-07.1-01 through 14-07.1-18.

Where to File: In District Court.

Temporary Ex Parte Orders: Yes. A full hearing must be held within 14 days.

Validity: The order is valid until terminated by the court.

Enforcement: Violations may be punished as contempt of court, Class A misdemeanors and Class C felonies.

OHIO

The Law: Ohio Revised Code Section 3113.31.

Where to File: In the Domestic Relations Division of the Court of Common Pleas.

Temporary Ex Parte Orders: Yes. A full hearing must be held within seven days.

Validity: Up to one year, or within 60 days of the filing of a petition for divorce.

Enforcement: Violations may be punished as contempt of court.

OKLAHOMA

The Law: Oklahoma Statutes Title 22, Section 60.1 through Section 60.8

Where to File: District Court

Temporary Ex Parte Orders: Yes. A full hearing must be held within ten days.

Validity: The order is valid until modified or terminated by the court.

Enforcement: Violations are punishable as misdemeanors.

OREGON

The Law: Oregon Revised Statutes Chapter 107, Section 700 through Section 730.

Where to File: Circuit Court

Temporary Ex Parte Orders: Yes. The court must order a hearing within 21 days of the respondent's request for a hearing.

Validity: Up to one year.

Enforcement: Violations are punishable as contempt of court.

PENNSYLVANIA

The Law: 23 Pennsylvania Consolidated Statutes Section 6101 through 6117.

Where to File: District Court, or Philadelphia Municipal Court.

Temporary Ex Parte Orders: Yes. A full hearing must be held within ten days.

Validity: Up to one year.

Enforcement: Violations are considered criminal contempt.

RHODE ISLAND

The Law: General Laws of Rhode Island Section 15-5-1 through 15-15-7.

Where to File: Family Court.

Temporary Ex Parte Orders: Yes. A full hearing must be held within 21 days.

Validity: Up to one year, then the court may extend the order for such additional time as it deems necessary.

Enforcement: Violations are considered misdemeanors.

SOUTH CAROLINA

The Law: Code of Laws of South Carolina Section 20-4-10 through Section 20-4-130.

Where to File: Family Court, or Magistrates Court if Family Court is not in session.

Temporary Ex Parte Orders: No. However, the court may hold an emergency hearing within 24 hours of service of the order.

Validity: Up to six months, then may be extended.

Enforcement: Violations are considered misdemeanors.

SOUTH DAKOTA

The Law: South Dakota Codified Laws Section 25-10-1 through 25-10-33.

Where to File: Circuit Court.

Temporary Ex Parte Orders: Yes. A full hearing must be held within 21 days.

Validity: Up to one year.

Enforcement: Violations are treated a Class One misdemeanors.

TENNESSEE

The Law: Tennessee Code Section 36-3-601 through 36-3-614.

Where to File: In the local court of record with jurisdiction over domestic relations matters.

Temporary Ex Parte Orders: Yes. A full hearing must be held within ten days.

Validity: Up to one year. The order may be extended for an additional year.

Enforcement: Violations are treated as civil or criminal contempt.

TEXAS

The Law: Texas Code, Family Section 71.01 through 71.19.

Where to File: In the District Court, Court of Domestic Relations, Juvenile Court or a County Court.

Temporary Ex Parte Orders: Yes, but they may not exceed 20 days.

Validity: Up to one year.

Enforcement: Violations may be treated as felonies.

UTAH

The Law: Utah Code Section 30-6-1 through 30-6-11.

Where to File: District Court or Juvenile Court.

Temporary Ex Parte Orders: Yes. A hearing must be held within 20 days.

Validity: Up to 120 days.

Enforcement: Violations are treated as class A misdemeanors.

VERMONT

The Law: Vermont Rules for Family Proceedings, Rule 9, and Vermont Statutes Section 15-1101 through 15-1109.

Where to File: District Court or Superior Court.

Temporary Ex Parte Orders: Yes. A full hearing must be held within ten days.

Validity: Up to one year, then it may be extended.

Enforcement: Violations are treated as criminal contempt.

VIRGINIA

The Law: Code of Virginia Section 16.1-253.1 et seq. and Section 16.1-279.1.

Where to File: Family Court.

Temporary Ex Parte Orders:? Yes. A full hearing must be held within 15 days.

Validity: Up to one year.

Enforcement: Violations are treated as Class One misdemeanors and contempt of court.

WASHINGTON

The Law: Revised Code of Washington, Title 26, Chapter 26.50.010 through 26.50.903.

Where to File: Superior Court, District Court or Municipal Court.

Temporary Ex Parte Orders: Yes. A full hearing must be held within 14 days.

Validity: Up to one year, then it may be extended.

Enforcement: Violations are treated as misdemeanors or contempt of court. If the violation is in the nature of an assault, it may be treated as a felony.

WEST VIRGINIA

The Law: West Virginia Code Section 48-2A-1 through Section 48-2A-11.

Where to File: Circuit Court or Magistrate's Court.

Temporary Ex Parte Orders: Yes. A full hearing must be held within five days.

Validity: Up to 60 days, or, until a final divorce order is entered.

Enforcement: Violations are considered contempt of court.

WISCONSIN

The Law: Wisconsin Statutes Section 813.12.

Where to File: Circuit Court or Tribal Court.

Temporary Ex Parte Orders: Yes. A full hearing must be held within seven days.

Validity: Up to two years.

Enforcement: Violations may result in fines or imprisonment

WYOMING

The Law: Wyoming Statutes Section 35-21-101 through 35-21-106.

Where to File: County or District Court.

Temporary Ex Parte Orders: Yes. A full hearing must be held within 72 hours.

Validity: Up to three months. It may be extended for additional three month periods.

Enforcement: Violations are treated as misdemeanors.

CHAPTER 9

WHEN CHILDREN ARE VICTIMS

Mary and Roger noticed a striking change in their seven year old's behavior. Samuel, normally eager to go to school, began pretending that he was sick in the mornings. At night he begged to be allowed to sleep with them, even though he had slept in his own room all his life. He frequently called out in the night, complaining of nightmares. When his teacher called and told them that Samuel was becoming disruptive in school, Mary and Roger decided to consult a child psychologist.

After several meetings, they were horrified to hear that the psychologist believed that Samuel had been sexually abused. A visit to the family doctor confirmed that there was physical evidence that Samuel had been sexually assaulted.

Samuel adamantly denied any abuse for several weeks. Then one night, he finally told his mother that he had been attacked on the way home from school. The person who assaulted him was a young man who lived a block from the school. After an investigation, the police arrested the man that Samuel identified, and now they are waiting for the trial. Mary and Roger feel that Samuel's ordeal is not yet over. They are very worried about the effect the court proceedings will have on him.

Samuel is extremely embarrassed and frightened each time he is asked about the attack. He has already given statements to his therapist, a child welfare worker, and a police detective. Each time that he is asked to relate the attack he becomes anxious and depressed, and his nightmares get worse. Now the prosecutor wants to interview him. Mary and Roger want to cooperate with the prosecution, but they wonder when this will end, and if they must allow Sam to submit to unlimited interviews.

Sam's parents may be able to get a court order protecting Samuel. Many adults who have been sexually attacked have a profound sense of shame and anxiety regarding the attack. This reaction is even more pronounced in children, who don't yet have the reasoning skills to help them deal with their feelings. Some very young victims don't even have the vocabulary to describe the attack or their feelings about it.

It is necessary for prosecutors and others to speak to child victims of sexual assault, in order to investigate, apprehend and convict the perpetrators of these crimes. But with each interview the child relives the trauma of the attack. For this reason, some states have passed laws that allow the court to limit the number of interviews that a child must undergo for the purpose of the investigation or prosecution. Alabama, Florida and West Virginia have such laws.

Other states direct that law enforcement officials cooperate to limit the number of interviews that a young victim must undergo, and conduct joint interviews whenever possible. Those states are New Hampshire, New York, and North Dakota.

Along similar lines, a Kentucky law directs the attorneys handling prosecutions involving minor victims to minimize the child's involvement in legal proceedings and avoid court appearances wherever possible.

When the case is filed, will Samuel's name be made part of the public record, for anyone to see?

Court records involving criminal prosecutions are usually open to the public, which means that the victim's name is available to anyone who looks at the complaint, information or indictment filed in the case. Some states have laws that are designed to protect the privacy of minor victims of sexual assault or other crimes:

- •In Alabama and Washington, records of court proceedings involving sexual crimes against children are kept confidential and are not open to the public.
- •In Iowa, Minnesota, New Jersey, North Dakota and Pennsylvania in cases involving sexual assault, physical abuse or neglect against children, the name, address or identity of the victim shall not appear in public records.
- •In Maine, law enforcement and prosecution personnel must refrain from any unnecessary pretrial public

disclosure of information that might identify the minor victim of a sexual offense.

- •In Rhode Island, public officials are prohibited from releasing the names of minors who are crime victims. Wyoming has a similar law that applies to minors who are victims of sexual offenses.
- •In the state of Washington, the child's name, address and photo may not be disclosed unless the child's parents grant permission for such disclosure.

Even under the best of circumstances, Samuel is shy when talking to strangers. What if he just clams up on the witness stand?

If Samuel refuses to say anything, he will probably be excused as a witness. Unfortunately, this may mean that the prosecution will fail.

Prosecuting crimes against children can be very difficult when the victim of the crime is the only witness. Every parent knows that their normally talkative child can become tongue tied when he or she is the center of attention. The serious nature and formality of court proceedings make it even more difficult for children to relate traumatic events. For this reason, many states have enacted laws which ease the restrictions normally imposed on lawyers who are questioning child witnesses.

One way in which states give those questioning child witnesses extra assistance is to allow the use of leading questions. If allowed to use "leading questions," the prosecutor can make it easier for Samuel to testify. Normally, court rules don't allow the lawyers in a case to ask leading questions during their direct examination.

Leading questions are the type of questions that "put words in the witness's mouth." For example, in a case involving a car accident, the plaintiff's lawyer might want Mrs. Smith to testify that she saw the blue car run the red light. He would be allowed to ask Mrs. Smith, "What did you see at the intersection?" He would not be allowed to ask "Didn't you see the blue car run the red light?" This is a leading question, and if Mrs. Smith was his witness, he would not be allowed to question her in that manner. (Leading questions are permitted during cross-examination, however.) Alabama and California allow the use of leading questions during direct examination of young witnesses. Additionally, California law provides that judges are to make sure that questions are asked in a form appropriate to the age of the witness.

In addition to the rules which allow leading questions, some states also provide that children and the lawyers questioning them, may make use of anatomically correct dolls to illustrate their testimony. This is very helpful if the child's verbal skills are limited, or if the child is too embarrassed to say certain words or verbally describe certain acts.

Some states provide that lawyers are to remain seating during the child's examination and cross examination, so that the child is not intimidated, and courts may direct that no one enter or exit the courtroom during the child's testimony. Some states go so far as to allow the judge to close the courtroom to the general public. (Many of these states, however, provide that members of the news media must be allowed to stay in the courtroom.)

Some state laws allow the judge to remove his or her robes in case the formal attire intimidates the child, and the courtroom may be rearranged to make the child more comfortable. The judge may also allow the child rest periods during his or her testimony. Many state laws allow a support person to be seated near the child while he or she testifies.

Is there an easier way for Samuel to give his evidence? Couldn't he tape his testimony ahead of time?

Yes, at least in some states, under some circumstances. Many states have enacted legislation that allows the child to give his or her testimony through a videotaped deposition. The videotape is then shown to the jury, instead of having the child on the witness stand, with the jury, court personnel and spectators looking on. These laws limit who may attend the videotaping, so that the child is not required to give frightening, perhaps embarrassing testimony before a room full of strangers and curious onlookers.

Of course, the defense has the right to be present and to cross examine the child, since otherwise the defendant's constitutional right to confront his or her accuser would be violated.

Under most state laws, the court must hold a hearing to determine if this type of deposition is necessary to protect the child victim or witness. Usually the court must consider factors such as the age and maturity of the child, the nature of the offense, the nature of the anticipated testimony, and the effect that giving such testimony in court may have on the child. The court must find that the child is likely to be unavailable to testify. Such a finding may be based on the testimony of a therapist that the child would suffer trauma if required to testify.

One state, New Hampshire, also provides for the use of a video-taped deposition if the delays that are inherent in criminal prosecutions would impair the child's ability to recall and relate the events that form the basis of the criminal complaint.

In the following states, the deposition is taken in the judge's presence, with the prosecutor, the defendant and his or her attorney, as well as any person necessary for the child's well-being: Alabama, Arkansas, Montana, Nebraska, New Hampshire, New Mexico, Tennessee and Wisconsin. In Alabama, the parents may have their own attorney present as well.

In the following states, the judge, the prosecutor and the defense attorney, as well as any person necessary for the child's well-being are present with the child. The defendant may be excluded from the room, or screened from the child's view if his or her presence would cause the child to be too intimidated to testify in a reliable manner: Connecticut, Florida, Iowa, Massachusetts, Minnesota, Mississippi (where the judge may also appoint a special master to preside at the deposition, and allow the child's therapist to assist with the questioning), Missouri, Nevada, Ohio, (the child must be provided with a monitor so that he or she may see the defendant while testifying) Pennsylvania, Rhode Island, South Dakota (the witness must be able to see the defendant on the monitor) Texas, Utah, Vermont and Wyoming.

In the following states, only the attorneys and any person necessary for the child's well-being are present: Kansas, Kentucky and Oklahoma.

In Indiana, the judge, lawyers and court reporter must all be hidden from the child's view during the videotaping.

California law provides that the testimony given by a young victim may be taped at the preliminary hearing, and then introduced at trial, in the place of the child's live testimony.

Samuel's therapist has videotaped all their sessions, including those in which he described the attack. Couldn't this tape be used instead of a deposition?

No, because the defendant has the right to cross-examine Sam. However, if the defendant has that chance, whether in the courtroom, or at a deposition, the court may allow the introduction of the tape as well. Some states have laws which allow the introduction of videotapes made of interviews with the child victim, as long as the tape wasn't made for the purpose of trial. For example, a taped therapy session, made before the investigation, in which Samuel describes the sexual assault to his counselor might be shown to the jury. Since such a videotape could be very prejudicial to the defendant, it must meet strict requirements before it may be shown to the judge or jury:

- The statement must have been made before the prosecution was commenced. This means before the grand jury returns an indictment, or before the prosecutor filed a complaint or information charging the crime.
- There must be no attorneys, either for the defense or the prosecution present.
- Every voice on the recording must be identified.
- The person who conducted the interview must be available to testify and be cross-examined at trial.
- The defense must have the opportunity to review the tape before trial.
- The child must be available to testify.
- The recording must be accurate and not altered in any way.
- The statement must not have been elicited by the use of leading questions.

The following states allow the introduction of such a tape: Arizona, Hawaii, Kansas, Kentucky, Louisiana, Missouri, Oklahoma, Texas and Utah.

Wisconsin allows the admission of a videotaped statement if the time, content and circumstances of the statement indicate that it is trustworthy.

The state of Texas has an additional provision in its laws. It allows the admission of an oral statement made by a child victim before a complaint is filed or an indictment returned. The statement may be admitted in a prosecution for a physical or sexual assault, or other crime of a sexual nature if the court finds that the factual issues were fully and fairly inquired into by a neutral person experienced in child abuse cases. Both the prosecution and the defense must be allowed to later give that person written questions to put to the child in another recorded session, and that session must also be offered into evidence at the trial.

Samuel's state doesn't allow videotaped testimony. Couldn't Sam just go into the judge's office, and tell the judge what happened?

The state of New Hampshire has a law that provides that in prosecutions for sexual assault, if the victim of the crime is under 16 years old, his or her testimony is to be given *in camera*. This means that the witness may testify in the judge's chambers, out of sight and hearing of the jury. The court reporter can then read his or her transcription of the testimony to the jury. If the defendant objects to this procedure, he or she must show good cause why the victim should be required to testify in the courtroom.

The states of Nebraska and Maine have similar provisions for young witnesses. In most states, however, this sort of procedure would not be allowed if the defendant is exercising his or her right to a jury trial.

However, Samuel might be able to give his evidence to the jury, without actually appearing in front of them. Because courtroom atmosphere and procedure can be so intimidating, some states have enacted laws that allow children to give their evidence from another room, such as the judge's office, through closed circuit television, or through the use of two way mirrors. The child is questioned by the prosecution and defense in that room and the testimony is televised by closed circuit television in the courtroom. The defendant might or might not be present in the room with the child, depending on the law in the state where the prosecution is being held, but the child is not facing a room full of spectators.

Every criminal defendant has the constitutional right to "confront" his or her accusers. For most of our history, this has meant that the defendant and the witnesses against him meet face to face in open court. The witness or victim must give his or her testimony in view of the defendant. The laws allowing the use of closed circuit testimony must be carefully drafted and applied, so that they do not deny the defendant his or her rights.

The court will decide before the trial if this type of set up is necessary. The court will consider the age and maturity of the child, the nature of the offense, the nature of the anticipated testimony, and the effect that giving such testimony in court may have on the child. The court may also consider any physical, psychological or emotional injury suffered by the child. In most states, the use of closed circuit technology is allowed if the child would suffer undue stress or psychological harm by being required to testify in the courtroom. In some states the court is directed to consider whether the child is unable to testify in the defendant's presence due to threats, or to the fact that the defendant occupies a position of authority over the child, due to the use of a deadly weapon during the crime, due to the infliction of injury during the crime, or due to the behavior of the defense counsel.

All states that allow the use of closed circuit television require that the persons in the room to operate the equipment be screened from the child's view, so that their presence does not distract or intimidate the child.

In the following states, the judge, the prosecutor and the defense attorney, as well as any person necessary for the child's well-being are present with the child. The defendant may be excluded from the room, or screened from the child's view if his or her presence would cause the child to be too intimidated to testify in a reliable manner: Connecticut, Florida, Georgia, Hawaii,

169

Louisiana, Massachusetts, Minnesota, Pennsylvania, Rhode Island, Texas and Utah.

In the following states, the prosecutor, the defendant and his or her attorney are in the room with the child. Any person necessary for the child's well-being may also be present: Alabama and South Dakota.

In Iowa, the judge, the defendant and counsel and the prosecutor are present, along with a person who would contribute to the well-being of the child.

In the following states, the prosecutor, the defense attorney and any person necessary for the child's well-being are present in the room with the child while he or she is testifying. The judge and the defendant remain in the courtroom, or in the alternative, the defendant must be screened from the child's view so that the child may neither hear nor see the defendant: Alaska, Arizona, Delaware, Kansas, Kentucky, Maryland, New Jersey, Ohio (in Ohio, the child must be provided with a monitor that allows him or her to see the defendant while testifying) Oklahoma, Virginia and Washington. The Washington statute allowing for closed circuit testimony requires that before it is allowed the prosecutor must show that she made reasonable efforts to prepare the child to testify in court, such as by referrals for counseling, a tour of the court, and an explanation of the trial process.

In California, Idaho, Indiana and Vermont the child is out of the presence of the judge, jury, defendant and the attorneys for the prosecution and defense, and the attorneys must question the child by television.

Samuel's therapist feels that giving evidence at the trial will be a threat to Sam's emotional stability. She had advised Mary and Roger to tell the prosecutor that he cannot testify. Could Mary testify in his place, and tell the jury what Samuel told her about the attack?

Mary's testimony would be what the courts call "hearsay," and in most circumstances hearsay testimony is not allowed. The defendant's right to confront his or her accusers is the reason that courts exclude hearsay testimony. Hearsay is defined as a statement made out of court, by an individual who is not present in court to be cross examined, that is offered to prove the truth of the matter asserted in the statement. In other words, if a witness comes to court and offers to testify regarding a statement that someone else made, the testimony is hearsay, and under most circumstances, not permitted in court.

Some states have passed laws that ease the prohibition against hearsay statements in prosecutions for sexual crimes against children. These laws allow witnesses to testify regarding statements made to them by the young victims. Under these laws, a witness can come to court and tell the jury that the child victim related the details of the crime to him or her. This is a dramatic departure from the usual rules of evidence, and has limited application. Most laws limit the application of this exception to the hearsay rule to young children, such as preteens. The court, under most statutes, must find that the child is unavailable to testify. Facts that would support a finding that the child is unavailable are:

• The death of the child.
• The fact that the defendant has hidden the child or removed the child from the jurisdiction of the court.
• The fact that the child is disabled, or unable to communicate.
• The fact that the child will suffer severe trauma if required to testify.

A prosecutor who wants to use an out of court statement may be required to present expert testimony to prove that the child is unavailable to testify. Some states require that there be other evidence that corroborates the hearsay statement, or that the statement possess "particularized guarantees of trustworthiness." The court might consider the following factors, taken from the Delaware child-victim hearsay law, in determining if the statement possesses these guarantees:

• The child's personal knowledge of the event.
• The age and maturity of the child.
• The credibility of the person reporting the statement.
• Whether the child has a motive to lie.
• The timing of the statement.

- •Whether the statement was heard by more than one person.
- •Whether the child was suffering any pain or distress when making the statement.
- •The nature and the duration of the alleged abuse.
- •If the child's young age makes fabrication unlikely.
- •If the statement has a "ring of verity"; that is, if it is internally consistent.
- •If the statement was spontaneous, or if it was elicited by leading questions.
- •If the extrinsic evidence shows that the defendant had the opportunity to commit the acts that he or she is accused of.

Along similar lines, Colorado law requires that the court find there is evidence that corroborates the child's statement, and that the time, content and circumstances of the statement provide sufficient safeguards of its reliability.

The following states allow the introduction of the child's out of court statement if the child will also testify in person, through a videotaped deposition or over closed circuit television or if the child is unavailable as a witness: Alabama, Arizona, Colorado, Delaware, Florida, Georgia, Idaho, Illinois, Kansas, Minnesota, Mississippi, Missouri, Nevada, Oklahoma, Pennsylvania, South Dakota, Texas, Utah, Vermont and Washington.

Maryland limits the application of its law to situations in which the statement was made to a professional involved with the child, such as the child's physician, psychologist, social worker or teacher. In a similar manner, the Mississippi law mandates that the statement must have been made for the purpose of receiving assistance or advice, and was made to a person the child should have reasonably relied on for such assistance.

Alaska allows the introduction of a child's out of court statement only at grand jury proceedings, if the circumstances under which the statement was made indicate that it is reliable, if there is additional evidence that corroborates the statement and if the child testifies at the grand jury proceeding or the child will be available to testify at trial.

California allows the introduction of hearsay in very limited circumstances: if it is given by a child under the age of 12 who is the victim of sexual abuse, and if that statement is included in a report made by law enforcement or welfare officials. The statement is admissible if the accused has confessed, if the statement was made prior to the confession, if the court finds that the statement is not unreliable and that the child is not available to testify.

Can Samuel have his own lawyer participate in the prosecution, to protect his rights?

In some states, the court can appoint a guardian ad litem for a young victim or witness. In most cases, the guardian ad litem is an attorney who undertakes to protect a child's rights during court proceedings. In other states a victim advocate might be allowed to participate in the proceedings to protect the child. The following states allow the court to appoint a guardian ad litem for a young victim or witness: Alaska, Florida, Iowa, North Dakota, Utah and Vermont.

Even if the court does not appoint a lawyer for Samuel, most states have laws that provide that in the case of a crime victim who is unable to assert his or her rights due to mental or physical disabilities, or due to the fact that he or she is a minor, a representative may be appointed to exercise those rights. The representative might be a family member, but it is not necessary, and in some cases could even be detrimental.

The following abilities, listed in the Arizona law providing for victim representatives, are important in a child victim representative:

- The willingness and ability to undertake working with and accompanying the minor victim through all proceedings, including criminal, civil and dependency proceedings.
- The willingness and ability to communicate with the minor victim.
- The willingness and ability to express the concerns of the minor to those authorized to come in contact with the minor as a result of the proceedings.

That law further provides that the representative shall accompany the minor victim to all proceedings and explain to him or her beforehand the nature of those proceedings, including what the minor will be asked to do, and stressing to the minor that he or she will be asked to tell the truth.

Colorado law provides that the courts should designate a person to act on the child victim's or child witness' behalf. That person should:

- Explain the legal proceedings to the child.
- Advise the judge regarding the child's ability to understand and cooperate in the proceedings.
- Assist the child and his or her family in coping with the emotional impact of the crime and the court proceedings.
- Advise the district attorney about the ability of the child witness to cooperate with the prosecution and regarding the potential effects of the proceeding on the child.

In juvenile court cases, the child involved is always represented by counsel or by a guardian ad litem.

Samuel and his family have been waiting with a great deal of apprehension for the trial to begin. They just received word from the prosecutor that the defendant is going to request that the case be put off for two more months. Samuel's parents want this ordeal behind them and their son. Is there anything that they can do?

Many victims' rights acts allow victims and witnesses to address the court, and express their opinions and/or objections regarding requests for continuances, even if the prosecution and defense agree on a new court date. Other states, such as Idaho, Missouri, New Hampshire and New Jersey, New York, North Dakota and Wisconsin mandate that cases involving children be given precedence on the court calendar and that the court must consider the impact of the delay on the young victim or witness when considering continuance requests.

Kentucky and Michigan law allow the prosecutor to request that cases involving minor victims or sexual or physical abuse be scheduled for a "speedy trial." Washington law prohibits continuances or delays of the case unless the court finds that there are compelling reasons for the continuance and that the benefits of the delay outweigh the harm to the victim.

Samuel's attacker has no previous convictions, and his parents are well-respected in the community. Mary and Roger want him to be punished if he is convicted. They want the judge to understand that the attacks on their child have robbed him of his innocence, and he will live with this violation every day of his life. Is there anything they can do?

Yes. Mary and Roger should prepare a victim impact statement on Samuel's behalf, and detail the effects that the crime have had on their child. They should consult with the prosecutor to see if they are allowed to incorporate statements or reports from Sam's counselor or experts in the field of child sexual abuse, to let the judge know the extent of the child's present pain, and the likely long term impact on his life.

States which allow the consideration of victim impact statements allow a victim representative to make the statement if the victim is unable to, due to death, youth or other disability. The state of Illinois specifically provides for the use of child impact statements in sentencing.

Suggestions for Parents of Children Who are Abused

Work with the police, prosecutors, and social workers to coordinate interviews. If the prosecutor can be present for a therapist's interview, for example, you might be able to minimize the number of times your child will be required to tell his or her story.

If your child has not been seeing a counselor, make at least one appointment with a therapist to evaluate the effect of the proceedings on him or her.

Ask the prosecutor about alternatives to giving testimony in open court, such as closed circuit testimony, or videotaped testimony.

Let the prosecutor know about any statements your child made to you, your state law might allow you to testify about those statements.

If your child will be taking the witness stand, discuss the setup of the courtroom with him or her, ask if you will be allowed to sit where your child can easily see you, if the lawyers will be ordered to keep their distance from your child, if the general public may be excluded during his or her testimony. Ask the prosecutor if you may bring your child to court when the court is not in session, to familiarize him or her with the courtroom.

State by State Summary of Laws Designed to Protect Young Victims

ALABAMA

Courts may limit the number of interviews a child victim under the age of 12 must undergo.

Records of court proceedings regarding sexual abuse or exploitation are not open to the public if the victim is under the age of 18.

Leading questions may be used when eliciting testimony from a victim or witness under the age of 10.

In prosecutions for sexual offenses against children the testimony of a victim or witness under the age of 16 may be taken by a videotaped deposition.

In prosecutions for sexual offenses against children the testimony of the victim or witness under the age of 16 may be given by closed circuit television.

In prosecutions for sexual offenses against children the out of court statement of a child under the age of 12 may be admitted into evidence.

ALASKA

The court may appoint a guardian ad litem for a child under the age of 13 who is the victim of, or a witness to crime.

In prosecutions for crimes against a person the testimony of a victim or witness under the age of 13 may be given by closed circuit television or two way mirrors.

The out of court statement of a child under the age of 10 may be introduced at the grand jury proceeding in prosecutions for sexual offenses.

ARIZONA

An audiovisual recording on film or videotape, made before the commencement of the prosecution, of an oral statement made by a minor victim or witness of a sexual assault be admitted into evidence at trial.

The testimony of a child victim or witness may be given over closed circuit television or by a videotaped deposition.

The out of court statement of a child victim or witness under the age of 10 may be introduced at trial, in prosecutions for sexual offenses or physical abuse.

ARKANSAS

The testimony of a victim under the age of 17 may be given by videotaped deposition.

In prosecutions involving a minor victim, the child's parents or guardians have the right to be present at all proceedings.

CALIFORNIA

Judges are directed to insure that questions are asked in a form appropriate to the witness' age.

The testimony of witnesses under the age of 10 may be elicited by the use of leading questions.

The testimony of a victim under the age of 15 may be taped at the preliminary hearing, and then introduced at trial, in place of live testimony.

The testimony of a victim under the age of 11 may be given over closed circuit television.

The out of court statements of a victim of sexual assault under the age of 12 may be admitted into evidence at trial.

COLORADO

The testimony of a victim of sexual assault who is under the age of 15 may be given through a videotaped deposition.

The out of court statements of a child under the age of 15 who is the victim of a sexual offense may be admitted at trial.

The courts and representative of law enforcement agencies are encouraged to designate an individual to act on behalf of children who are involved in criminal proceedings, either as witnesses or victims.

CONNECTICUT

The court may prohibit people from entering or leaving the court room during a child's testimony, may require that the attorneys remain seated during their questioning of the child, may allow a supportive adult to sit near the child during his or her testimony and may allow the child to use dolls to illustrate his or her testimony.

The testimony of a child under the age of 12 may be given by videotaped deposition.

The testimony of a child under the age of 12 may be given by closed circuit television.

DELAWARE

The testimony of a witness under the age of 11 may be given by closed circuit television.

The out of court statements of a child victim under the age of 11 may be introduced in evidence in prosecutions involving physical or sexual abuse.

FLORIDA

The testimony of a victim or witness under the age of 16 may be given by a videotaped deposition in prosecutions for child abuse or sexual abuse.

The testimony of a victim or witness under the age of 16 may be given by closed circuit television in prosecutions for child abuse or sexual abuse.

The court is required to appoint a guardian ad litem for a minor who is a victim of or witness to abuse or a sexual offense.

The court may enter orders to limit or prohibit interviews of a child victim.

The court may clear the courtroom of persons not necessary to the prosecution during the testimony of a minor under the age of

16, if that testimony is regarding a sexual offense. (However, the court may not bar representatives of the news media.)

The out of court statements of a victim 11 years of age or under may be admitted in prosecutions for abuse, sexual abuse or neglect.

GEORGIA

The out of court statements of a child under the age of 14 may be admitted in prosecutions for physical or sexual abuse.

The testimony of a witness under the age of 10 may be given by closed circuit television.

The judge may clear the courtroom of all spectators, with the exception of reporters, during the testimony of a victim under the age of 16 testifying with regard to a sexual offense.

HAWAII

The testimony of a victim under the age of 16 may be given by closed circuit television in prosecutions for sexual offenses or child abuse.

A statement of a victim under the age of 16, recorded prior to the commencement of the prosecution may be introduced into evidence in prosecutions for child abuse or sexual offenses.

Witnesses under the age of 14 may have a parent, counselor or other adult nearby during his or her testimony.

IDAHO

Children who are witnesses may have a support person in the courtroom, and by the witness stand during their testimony.

The out of court statements of a victim under the age of 10 may be admitted into evidence in prosecutions for physical or sexual abuse.

The testimony of a child under the age of 16 may be given by closed circuit television in prosecutions for sexual offenses or ritualized abuse.

The courts must attempt to insure a speedy trial in cases involving a child victim or witness and consider the impact of delay on the child when considering an application for a continuance.

ILLINOIS

The out of court statements of a child under the age of 13 may be admitted into evidence in prosecutions for child abuse or unlawful sexual activity.

179

The court may clear the courtroom of all spectators without a direct interest in the case during the testimony of a minor under the age of 16 who is the victim of a sexual offense. (However, the court may not bar reporters.)

INDIANA

The testimony of a victim under the age of 14 may be given by closed circuit television.

The testimony of a victim under the age of 14 may be given by videotaped deposition.

IOWA

The identity of a minor victim of a sexual assault is not to be released to the public prior to the filing of an information or indictment against a suspect. The child's name or other identifying information shall not appear on any public records after the charges are filed or the indictment issued.

The testimony of a minor victim may be given by closed circuit television.

The testimony of a minor victim may be given by videotaped deposition.

The court may limit the duration of a minor victim's testimony.

The court shall appoint a guardian ad litem for a minor victim.

KANSAS

The out of court statement of a minor victim may be admitted into evidence in a prosecution for sexual offenses

A statement of a victim under the age of 13, videotaped prior to the commencement of the criminal prosecution may be admitted into evidence at trial.

The testimony of a victim under the age of 13 may be given by videotaped deposition.

The testimony of a victim under the age of 13 may be given by closed circuit television.

KENTUCKY

A statement of a child under the age of 13, videotaped prior to the commencement of the criminal prosecution may be admitted into evidence at trial for sexual offenses.

The testimony of a child under the age of 13 may be given by closed circuit television in prosecutions for sexual offenses.

The testimony of a child under the age of 13 may be given by a videotaped deposition in prosecutions for sexual offenses.

The attorneys should attempt to minimize the child's involvement in legal proceedings, avoiding unnecessary court appearances.

In prosecutions for sexual offenses against victims under the age of 16, a speedy trial may be scheduled, and the court must consider the impact of delay on the child when considering a request for a continuance.

LOUISIANA

The testimony of a victim under the age of 14 may be given by closed circuit television in prosecutions for physical or sexual abuse.

The testimony of a victim under the age of 14 may be given by videotaped deposition in prosecutions for physical or sexual abuse.

A videotaped statement made by a minor victim prior to the commencement of the proceedings may be admitted into evidence at trial.

In prosecutions for sexual assault, the testimony of a victim under the age of 16 may be given in closed session.

MAINE

The out of court statements of a child under the age of 16 may be admitted in prosecutions for unlawful sexual acts.

Prosecutors and law enforcement personnel must refrain from any unnecessary pretrial public disclosure of information that might identify the minor victim of a sexual offense.

MARYLAND

The out of court statements of a victim under the age of 12 may be admitted in prosecutions for child abuse, child neglect or sexual offenses.

The testimony of a minor victim may be given by closed circuit television.

MASSACHUSETTS

The testimony of a minor under the age of 15 may be given by videotaped deposition.

181

The testimony of a minor under the age of 15 may be given by closed circuit television.

The court shall exclude the public from the courtroom during prosecutions for sexual offenses against victims under the age of 18.

MICHIGAN

A speedy trial may be scheduled for cases in which the victim is the victim of child abuse, including child sexual abuse.

Children under the age of 15 (and older children who have developmental disabilities) may use dolls or mannequins to illustrate their testimony, they may also have a support person nearby during their testimony.

All persons who are not necessary to the proceeding may be excluded from the courtroom during a child's testimony at the preliminary hearing and at trial. If the court follows this procedure at trial, the judge must arrange to have the child's testimony broadcast, over closed circuit television, to the public in another part of the courthouse.

The court may order that the defendant be seated as far away as possible from the child during his or her preliminary hearing testimony, and during the trial.

The police may take the videotaped statement of a child to use during preliminary proceedings (but not during the preliminary hearing) for impeachment purposes, and for use during sentencing. The testimony of a child victim under the age of 15 (or older if he or she has developmental disabilities) may be taken by videotaped deposition.

MINNESOTA

The out of court statement of a child under the age of 10 (or a person of any age who is mentally impaired) may be admitted in prosecutions for sexual offenses or physical abuse.

The testimony of a minor victim under the age of 12 may be given by closed circuit television, in prosecutions for physical abuse or sexual offenses.

The testimony of a minor victim under the age of 12 may be given by a videotaped deposition, in prosecutions for physical abuse or sexual offenses.

The public may not have access to information in police reports which identifies a minor who is the victim of a crime.

The public may be excluded from the courtroom during the testimony of a minor under the age of 18 who is the victim of a sexual assault.

A victim under the age of 18 may have a support person present during the trial, even if that person is also scheduled to testify, unless the presence of that person would create a substantial risk of influencing testimony.

MISSISSIPPI

The out of court statement of a child under the age of 12, may be admitted in prosecutions for child abuse or sexual abuse.

A victim under the age of 16 may testify by closed circuit television in prosecutions for sexual offenses.

A victim under the age of 16 may testify by videotaped deposition.

MISSOURI

The testimony of a witness under the age of 17 may be given through a videotaped deposition.

Cases involving child victims or witnesses are given priority on the court calendar. The court must consider the well-being of the child when ruling on a motion for continuance.

The out of court statements of a child under the age of 12 may be introduced into evidence at trial.

The previously recorded statement of a child made before the commencement of the proceedings may be admitted into evidence.

MONTANA

The testimony of a victim under the age of 16 may be given through a videotaped deposition.

NEBRASKA

The testimony of a child under the age of 12 may be given through a videotaped deposition or in the judge's chambers.

NEVADA

The out of court statements of children under the age of 10 may be admitted into evidence at trial for a sexual offenses.

Any witness under the age of 14, or a person of any age who is the victim of a sexual assault may give his or her testimony through a videotaped deposition.

NEW HAMPSHIRE

The testimony of sexual assault victims under the age of 16 shall be heard in the judge's chambers, out of view and hearing of the jury, unless the defendant can show good cause why it should not be.

In sexual assault cases involving victims under the age of 14, the court must insure a speedy trial and consider the impact of delay on the victim when considering a request for a continuance.

The testimony of a child under the age of 17 may be given by videotaped deposition.

Law enforcement officials are directed to cooperate to limit the number of interviews required of young victims, and to conduct joint interviews where possible.

NEW JERSEY

The testimony of a child victim under the age of 17 may be given over closed circuit television in prosecutions for physical abuse or sexual offenses.

In cases involving a victim under the age of 14, the court should take action to insure a speedy trial, and when deciding an application for continuance, consider the effect on the child.

In cases involving sexual assault, physical abuse or neglect against children, the name, address or identity of the victim shall not appear in public records.

A child under the age of 16 may use dolls or models to illustrate his or her testimony.

NEW MEXICO

The testimony of a victim under the age of 16 may be given by a videotaped deposition in a prosecution for a sexual offense.

NEW YORK

Law enforcement officials shall cooperate to minimize the number of interviews required of a young victim.

Courts should consider the impact of the delay on young victims when considering applications for continuances.

The court should allow a support person to be with the child when he or she testifies.

A child witness should be allowed to use dolls or drawings to illustrate his or her testimony.

The testimony of a child under the age of 12 may be given by closed circuit television.

If a child under the age of 12 cannot understand the nature of the oath, the court may allow him or her to give unsworn testimony.

NORTH CAROLINA

The parent or guardian of a child who is a witness may be present for the child's testimony, even if that adult is also a witness in the case.

NORTH DAKOTA

The testimony of a victim under the age of 15 may be given by videotaped deposition in prosecutions for sexual offenses.

The court may appoint a guardian ad litem for a minor victim of a sexual offense.

Children should be provided with explanations of all legal proceedings in which they are involved, a representative of the child should advise the court regarding the child's ability to participate in court proceedings and the effects of the proceedings on the child, the child's family should be provided with referrals to appropriate social services, and child development specialists should be available to ensure that the questions asked of the child are appropriate to the child's age and development.

The name of a minor victim, and other identifying information shall not appear in any public record.

Law enforcement personnel must attempt to limit the number of interviews required of a child victim or witness.

The court shall attempt to insure a speedy trial in cases involving child victims or witnesses. When considering any continuance request, the court must consider the effect of delay on the young victim or witness.

A witness under the age of 14 may have a support person nearby during his or her testimony.

In some cases, the court may close the courtroom during the testimony of the child.

OHIO

The testimony of a victim under the age of 11 may be given by videotaped deposition in prosecutions for sexual offenses.

The testimony of a victim under the age of 11 may be given by closed circuit television in prosecutions for sexual offenses.

A videotape of the testimony of a victim under the age of 11 may be admitted into evidence instead of live testimony at trial.

OKLAHOMA

A statement of a child under the age of 13, videotaped prior to the commencement of the criminal prosecution, may be admitted into evidence at trial.

The testimony of a victim under the age of 13 may be given by closed circuit television.

The testimony of a victim under the age of 13 may be given by videotaped deposition.

The out of court statement of a victim under the age of 13 may be admitted in prosecutions for sexual offenses or physical abuse.

Witnesses under the age of 13 are allowed to have a support person present during their testimony.

OREGON

In cases involving children under the age of 18 as victims or witnesses, the court shall expedite the matter and insure it takes precedence over other cases. When considering a continuance request, the court shall consider the potential adverse impact of delay on the child.

A child under the age of 13 may be accompanied by a parent, guardian, or other appropriate adult during an appearance before a grand jury.

PENNSYLVANIA

The testimony of a child under the age of 14, and in most cases, aged 14 or 15, may be given by closed circuit television.

The testimony of a child under the age of 14, and in most cases, aged 14 or 15 may be given by videotaped deposition.

A child advocate may be appointed to provide services for children who are victims or witnesses.

The out of court statement of a child under the age of 13 may be admitted in prosecutions for sexual offenses.

In prosecutions for sexual offenses, the court shall permit a child to use dolls to assist his or her testimony.

The names of child victims of sexual offenses or physical abuse shall not be disclosed, and records that identify the child are not open to the public.

RHODE ISLAND

A recording of the statement made by a child victim who is under the age of 14 may be introduced in grand jury proceedings.

The testimony of a victim of sexual assault who is under the age of 18 may be given by videotaped deposition.

The testimony of a victim of sexual assault who is under the age of 18 may be given by closed circuit television.

In actions involving child victims under the age of 15, when considering a request for delay or continuance the court must consider the effect of the delay on the child.

Child victims under the age of 15 have the right to explanations of all proceedings, to the presence of a support person, to have proceedings so arranged as to minimize the time that the child must be present in court and to be permitted to testify in a manner which would be the least traumatic.

No member of any municipal or state agency may release the identity of any minor who is believed to be a victim of crime without the consent of the child's parents or guardians. A person who violates this law may be sued in civil court for damages.

SOUTH CAROLINA

Courts shall treat children with sensitivity, using closed or taped sessions where appropriate.

SOUTH DAKOTA

The out of court statement of a child under the age of 10, or over the age of 10, who is developmentally disabled, may be admitted in a trial for a sexual offense or for physical abuse or neglect.

The testimony of a child under the age of 12, or over the age of 12, who is developmentally disabled, may be given by closed circuit television in proceedings regarding sexual assault, physical abuse or neglect.

The court may close proceedings to the general public during a minor's testimony regarding a sexual offense.

The testimony of a victim under the age of 16, of a sexual offense, may be taken by videotaped deposition, or may be videotaped at the preliminary hearing.

TENNESSEE

The testimony of a child under the age of 13 may be given by videotaped deposition, in prosecutions for sexual offenses.

TEXAS

The testimony of a child under the age of 13 may be given by closed circuit television in a prosecution for a sexual offense, or for physical abuse.

The court may set any appropriate limits on taking a child's testimony.

The testimony of a child under the age of 13 may be given by videotaped deposition in a prosecution for a sexual offense or physical abuse.

The recording of an oral statement made by a child under the age of 13 made before the commencement of the prosecution may be admitted into evidence.

The out of court statement of a child under the age of 13 may be admitted into evidence in prosecutions for sexual or assaultive offenses.

UTAH

The out of court statement of a child victim under the age of 14 may be admitted into evidence in prosecutions for sexual abuse.

The court may appoint a guardian ad litem to represent a child alleged to be the victim in child abuse, child neglect or child sexual abuse proceedings.

The recording of an oral statement made by a victim or witness under the age of 14, made prior to the commencement of the prosecution, may be admitted into evidence involving child abuse or child sexual abuse.

The testimony of a victim or witness under the age of 14 may be given by closed circuit television in prosecutions for child abuse or child sexual abuse.

The testimony of a victim or witness under the age of 14 may be given through a videotaped deposition in prosecutions for child abuse or child sexual abuse.

Children have the right to be given a clear explanation of and to be assisted with their role in the criminal justice process.

Children have the right to a speedy disposition of any case they are involved in.

VERMONT

The court may appoint a guardian ad litem for a minor who is the victim of a sexual assault or other sexual offense.

The out of court statement of a child under the age of 11 may be admitted in a prosecution for sexual assault, other sexual offenses or physical abuse or neglect.

The testimony of a child under the age of 13 may be given by closed circuit television in a prosecution for sexual assault, other sexual offenses or physical abuse or neglect.

The testimony of a child under the age of 13 may be given by videotaped deposition in a prosecution for sexual assault, other sexual offenses or physical abuse or neglect.

VIRGINIA

The testimony of a child under the age of 13 may be given by closed circuit television in prosecutions for kidnapping, sexual offenses or family offenses.

WASHINGTON

The out of court statement of a child under the age of 10 may be admitted into evidence in prosecutions for sexual offenses.

The testimony of a child under the age of 10 may be given by closed circuit television in prosecutions for sexual offenses or physical abuse.

The child has the right to have legal proceedings and police investigations explained in easily understood language.

The child has the right to a secure waiting area and to have an advocate or support person close by at all times.

The child has the right to not have his or her name, address or photograph released without his or her guardian's permission.

The child has the right to have an advocate advise the prosecutor and the court about his or her ability to participate in the proceedings.

Any part of court records identifying a minor victim of a sexual assault are sealed and not open to public inspection.

The trial of sexual offenses against a minor may not be continued unless the court finds that the benefit of postponement outweighs the detriment to the victim.

WEST VIRGINIA

The court may limit the number of interviews that a child under the age of 12 may be required to submit to in a prosecution for a sexual offense.

WISCONSIN

The videotaped statement of a child under the age of 12 (and in some cases, up to the age of 16), may be admitted into evidence.

The testimony of a child under the age of 12 (and in some cases, up to the age of 16) may be taken by videotaped deposition.

The court should insure a speedy trial in cases involving young victims or witnesses. When considering a continuance request the court must consider the effect that delay will have on the wellbeing of the child.

The child has the right to an explanation of the legal proceedings that he or she will be involved in.

The child has the right to have an advocate advise the prosecutor and the judge regarding the child's ability to participate in the proceedings.

The child has the right to referrals to appropriate social services.

WYOMING

The testimony of a victim under the age of 12 may be taken by videotaped deposition in prosecutions for incest or sexual assault.

The name of a minor victim of indecent liberties, sexual assault or incest shall not be disclosed. Persons guilty of a wilful violation of this law are subject to a fine and incarceration.

CHAPTER 10

VICTIMS' RIGHTS TO PRIVACY

Lynette and David started going steady when they were sophomores in high school. When it came time for their senior prom, they were looking forward to a very special occasion. David cleaned and waxed his new pickup truck and Lynette's mother allowed her to borrow her diamond earrings.

After the dance, they went out to an all night diner with a group of their friends. Unfortunately, in the parking lot of the diner were two recently paroled convicts looking for someone to rob. When Lynette and David left the diner around 2:30 A.M., they seemed like perfect marks, too young and exhilarated to be careful about their surroundings and safety.

The convicts guessed correctly that the two teenagers might be headed for a secluded spot where they would find some privacy. The two men drove behind them through town, and watched them turn on to a little used county road that ended at a rock quarry.

The men turned their car lights off and drove slowly up the road. Lynette and David didn't hear them until the men were at the windows of the truck. At gunpoint, the men robbed the young couple of their jewelry and the little money that they had with them. They then forced them into the woods by the quarry where they tortured and sexually assaulted both Lynette and David. They tied their victims up and left them in the woods, then returned to the quarry. One assailant left in his own car, while the other stole David's truck.

Lynette and David had agreed to meet their friends at a breakfast hosted by their school. When they didn't appear, their friends and family became worried. When one of David's friends found David's truck abandoned in a convenience store parking lot, the Sheriff instituted a search. One of Lynette's friends suggested that they might have gone to the quarry, and the teens were located there that evening, suffering from exposure and dehydration, but still alive.

Neither of the parolees appeared the next week for their regular meetings with their parole officers, and warrants were issued for their arrest. When one of them was apprehended, he was wearing David's class ring. He also had a pawn ticket that showed that he had pawned the diamond earrings Lynette had been wearing. The teens both identified the parolee as one of their attackers, and the police knew that the description that they gave of the other matched one of his known associates, who was soon arrested. Now David and Lynette are waiting to testify at their assailants' trials.

Both David and Lynette are experiencing nightmares, panic attacks, and are having trouble with their friends and family. Lynette's parents have contacted a therapist, but Lynette is afraid to talk to her. She fears that her therapist might be called to testify at trial about the things that they have discussed. Should she wait until the trial is over before she begins counseling?

No. Lynette shouldn't wait to begin her counseling. It is very unlikely that anything she shares with her therapist would be relevant to any issue in the criminal trial. Additionally, many states have laws that guarantee the confidentiality of communications between crime victims and victim counselors. They work in much the same way as laws that protect the confidentiality of private communications between doctors and their patients. Most such laws apply to communications between the victims of domestic violence or sexual offenses and their counselors. Even states that don't have specific victim-counselor confidentiality laws may offer protection by making communications between psychologists and their clients confidential.

There are some exceptions to these laws. For example, victims or counselors might be compelled, under certain statutes, to testify regarding their confidential communications if those communications involved suspected child abuse or neglect. A crime victim cannot seek the counselor's assistance in planning a crime or escaping detection or apprehension after a crime and keep those communications private. If the counselor knows that the victim plans to commit perjury, some statutes require that he or she report it. Additionally, the victim-counselor privilege only covers communications, and doesn't extend to things like physical appearance. So a counselor might be compelled to testify about bruises or other obvious injuries the victim suffered.

The victim may waive the protection of the law, and allow the counselor to testify. For example, a rape victim might allow her counselor to testify that she exhibited symptoms of the rape trauma syndrome, in order to help the prosecution of the case.

On a related topic, some states have laws which specifically prohibit a court from ordering a crime victim or a witness to undergo a psychiatric or psychological examination to evaluate his or her credibility. Those states are Arizona, Idaho, and Illinois (the Illinois law pertains only to the victims of sex crimes).

The following states have laws that protect the confidentiality of communications between some crime victims (usually the victims of domestic violence or sexual assault) and victim counselors: Alabama, Alaska, Arizona, California, Connecticut, Florida, Hawaii, Illinois, Indiana, Iowa, Kentucky, Louisiana, Maine, Massachusetts, Michigan, Minnesota, New Hampshire, New Jersey, New Mexico, Pennsylvania and Utah.

After Lynette and David were rescued, they were interviewed at a detective's desk, in full view and within the hearing of any person who came by. Their parents wanted to know if anything could be done to prevent this in the future.

In Louisiana and New York, law enforcement officials are required to provide a private setting for interviewing victims, such as an enclosed room where the occupants are not visible nor their voices audible to those outside.

In other states, there is no legal requirement that victims be provided a private interview room, but good police procedure would seem to mandate it. Crime victims should insist that they be treated with the respect and compassion that they are due, and request that interviews take place in a private and dignified atmosphere. In appropriate circumstances, victims could request that interviews take place in their home, in the home of a friend, or in the office of a trusted professional, such as a minister, counselor or attorney.

Even though the men who attacked them are in jail, both David and Lynette fear that they will escape and attack or even kill them. Is there anyway that they can prevent the defendants from learning their names, or where they live?

Under most circumstances, if criminal defendants don't already know the identity of their victims, or learn them during the perpetration of the crime, they learn them when they are charged. This is because under most state laws, the prosecutor is required to list his or her witnesses on the document that states the charges against the accused. (This document is usually called an information or indictment.) In some states, the prosecutor is required to list the address of each witness as well. However, under some state laws, such as Colorado's, the prosecutor may obtain a court order that certain victims or witnesses names and addresses be withheld from the defendant.

In court proceedings, witnesses are routinely asked to state their address. However, many states provide that victims need not reveal their business and residence addresses when testifying, unless it is absolutely necessary.

An investigator for the defendants' attorney called David's father and wanted to arrange a time to interview David. Must they talk to the defense attorney?

No. If the defense has the right, under state law, to take the victim's deposition, the defense should set it up through the prosecutor's office. In most states, there is no legal requirement that prosecution witnesses speak to the defendants or their attorneys, or give depositions. Some states even have statutes which state that the victim has the right to refuse to speak with the defendant or counsel for the defense. Wyoming law allows the victim to refuse to speak to anyone.

If the victim is willing to grant an interview, he or she may set the conditions. For example, the victim may have the prosecutor and his or her own attorney present, may set the time and place, and may terminate the interview at any time.

Because of the sexual nature of the crime against them, both Lynette and David are hoping that the local media will not publish their identities. Do they have the right to keep their names out of documents that reporters will see, and can they legally prevent their identities from being revealed?

In cases involving sexual assault, most newspapers and radio and television stations voluntarily refrain from publishing the names of the victims even if it is not required by law. However, in a few states, the victim's name is not a part of the public record and may not be divulged.

Not every state has laws designed to protect victim privacy. Among those that do, the provisions vary dramatically from state to state. For information regarding the privacy rights of children who are the victims of crime, or regarding the privacy rights of the victims of sexual assault, see chapters 9 and 7.

Laws That Protect a Victim's Identity

ALASKA

The residence and business address and telephone numbers of a crime victim are confidential and any documents that contain this information may not be made available to the public unless those references are deleted.

The prosecution may withhold the victim's address and telephone number from the defendant, unless the defendant is acting as his or her own attorney. The prosecution may be required to furnish defense counsel with the victim's address and telephone number, but the court may order that it not be divulged to the defendant.

If the defendant's attorney or any other person representing the defendant contacts the victim, that person must inform the victim of his or her relationship to the defendant, that the victim need not speak to him or her and that the prosecutor or another person of the victim's choosing, may be present during any interview.

A victim may not be required to testify regarding his or her residence or business address and telephone numbers unless the court determines that information is necessary and relevant to the facts of the case.

The portion of court or police records that contain the victim's name is not a public record and should be withheld from public inspection except with the consent of the court. In open records, the victim's initials shall be used.

ARIZONA

A victim or witness may refuse to testify regarding his or her address, telephone number or place of employment unless there is a compelling need for that information.

A victim has the absolute right to refuse an interview, a deposition or other discovery request by the defendant, the defendant's attorney or any person acting for the defendant.

A victim has the right to require that the prosecutor withhold, during discovery and other proceedings, his or her home address and telephone number, the address and telephone number of his or her place of employment, and the name of the victim's employer, unless the court finds that there is good cause for defense counsel to have this information.

All defense requests to interview the victim must be made through the prosecutor's office.

Should the victim agree to an interview, he or she may specify a reasonable date, time, duration and location. He or she may terminate the interview if it is not conducted in a professional manner.

COLORADO

A court may order that the names and addresses of witnesses not be disclosed to the defendant by his or her attorney.

CONNECTICUT

Victims of sexual assault need not divulge their addresses in open court.

DELAWARE

The victim's address and telephone number, maintained by the court and law enforcement is *not* subject to disclosure pursuant to the Freedom of Information Act.

INDIANA

The victim is not required to testify regarding his or her residential address, telephone number, or place of employment if such disclosure would present a danger to the victim or the victim's family.

MARYLAND

The trial court judge may prohibit the release of the address or telephone number of any victim or witness.

MICHIGAN

If the victim has a reasonable apprehension of acts or threats of physical violence or intimidation the prosecutor may move that the victim not be compelled to testify regarding his or her address, place of employment, or other personal identification.

MINNESOTA

A victim has the right to request that a law enforcement agency withhold public access to data revealing his or her identity.

The victim may not be compelled, in court proceedings, to testify regarding his or her home or work address, unless the court finds that such testimony would be relevant evidence.

NEW HAMPSHIRE

The victim has the right to confidentiality regarding his or her address and place of employment.

NEW MEXICO

The victim need not testify regarding his or her address, place of employment or telephone number unless it is necessary to identify the scene of the crime.

NORTH CAROLINA

A victim or witness should be informed that his or her home address is not relevant in every case, and that he or she may request that the prosecutor raise an objection if that information is sought during the trial.

NORTH DAKOTA

A victim or witness may not be compelled to testify regarding his or her address, telephone number, place of employment or other personal identification, unless there is a showing of good cause as determined by the court.

OKLAHOMA

The court may order that the victim's address, telephone number and place of employment not be disclosed in court records or documents.

OREGON

The court may order that the victim's address and telephone number not be given to the defendant.

If contacted by the defense, the defense attorney must identify himself or herself and inform the victim that the victim is not required to speak with the defense counsel and that the victim may request that the prosecutor be present for any interview.

TEXAS

A victim's address may be included in the court file only if it is necessary, and the victim's phone number may not appear in the court file.

A victim of sexual assault may choose to be identified in all public records by a pseudonym and may choose not to divulge his or her address or telephone number.

UTAH

Victims and witnesses may not be required to state their addresses and telephone numbers in open court.

VIRGINIA

A judge may prohibit testimony regarding the victim's current address or telephone number.

WISCONSIN

A victim need not testify regarding his or her address or telephone number or place of employment unless that information is relevant to the proceedings.

WYOMING

The victim has the right to refuse to speak to investigators, attorneys, or law enforcement, unless he or she is on the witness stand, under oath.

INDEX